W9-AOI-975

Gerld Pchmidt

INDIAN PRIMITIVE

INDIAN PRIMITIVE

by

RALPH W. ANDREWS

Makah Whaler with Harpoon and
Sealskin Floats

EDWARD L. CURTIS PHOTO COURTESY
CHARLES E. LAURIAT CO.

BONANZA BOOKS · NEW YORK

© MCMLX, BY RALPH W. ANDREWS

All Rights Reserved

Library of Congress Catalog Card Number 60-14425

This edition published by Bonanza Books,
a division of Crown Publishers, Inc.,
by arrangement with Superior Publishing Company.

(B)

PRINTED IN THE UNITED STATES OF AMERICA

DEDICATED

to all those curious people

who were not there

FOREWORD

IN the former days there were some twenty-six Indian tribes living in the coastal area between Trinidad Bay in Northwestern California and Alaska's Yakutat Bay. Fifty or more books, involving years of painstaking research and contact with the remnants of these tribes, have been prepared by anthropologists and ethnologists.

All these books detail the differing tribal languages, life and customs, some containing fascinating accounts by explorers, pioneers and captives who saw the Indians as they lived in the latter days. All the references listed at the end of this volume are recommended to those wishing to study the subject.

Indian Primitive, however, is an attempt to portray many of these people as they lived before those we consider "white men" began to interfere with their singular lives. Since it is primarily a pictorial book and produced solely for information and entertainment rather than scientific study, it becomes of a popular and highlighted nature.

I have studied exhaustively and offer here my own personal conceptions and ideas of how the Indians lived, their childlike yet pagan natures, their crafts and their proud ancestral heritages. There was no photography in the pre-white era but many of the scenes and portraits I have used were taken by pioneers and early professional photographers, a few of whom recorded some rare activities and re-created some remarkable situations.

For invaluable help in obtaining photographs I am indebted to the several library and archive sources mentioned in the picture credit lines and to many individuals, among them—Mrs. Fred J. Meamber, Jr. of Siskiyou County Historical Society, Yreka, California; Mrs. Stanley B. Roscoe of Humboldt County Historical Society, Eureka, California; Mrs. Leona B. Hammond, Crescent City, California.

RALPH W. ANDREWS

CONTENTS

Coast Salish

DENSE forests of cedar, fir, hemlock and spruce fringed the waterways and blanketed the lands between them from Bute Inlet to Puget Sound. On these shores of inlets and rivers lived the several groups of Indians known as the Coast Salish. With footholds and antecedents in the interiors east of the mountain ranges, these tribes acquired much of the advanced culture of the Northern Indians, each Salish segment showing many variations in living customs.

In the lands now classified as British Columbia there were four main language groups: the Comox, midway along the East Coast of Vancouver Island; the Cowichan, south of the Comox on the same island and on parts of the Fraser River delta; the Sanetch on the southern tip of Vancouver Island and some areas of the mainland near the present site of the city of Vancouver; the Squamish, on the lower reaches and delta of the Fraser.

These were the tribes that accepted friendly tokens of trade when the big canoes of the Nootkas came bearing down the Strait of Juan de Fuca and passed up around the myriad islands in the Gulf of Georgia. And there were many more tribes to the South should the travelers decide to enter Puget Sound. These Nootka traders would find plenty of Indians, none talking their own language, and few of the home tribes being able to understand each other. The Nootkas might stay in one Salish village long enough to learn the simple words, enough to lavish gifts upon some chief who had a marriageable daughter, but when they journeyed on they at once found another strange tribe and had to start learning new words.

Here were the sheltered arms of the ocean and the open waters of the gulfs. Here also were the river mouths and the creeks running off the mountains and high banks. All of them were teeming with salmon around which was centered the whole food economy of the Coast Salish.

North of the Fraser River, the Comox, Cowichan and Sanetch people were blessed with a wide range of sea foods from smelt and herring to octopus and from sea urchins to clams. But even they, like the Squamish around the mouth of the Fraser, harvested the ever-present salmon in fabulous numbers as their staff of life. As long as the men could catch salmon and the women could dry it, the villages prospered and the tribe was strong.

Nootka Spearing Salmon

EDWARD L. CURTIS PHOTO COURTESY
CHARLES E. LAURIAT CO.

There were five species of salmon spawning in this area at slightly different seasons and full advantage was taken to trap them in the river shallows. The weirs were crude but they caught fish. Cedar slats or small poles were pounded into the river bed a few inches apart to form a solid row from bank to bank. An opening was left—perhaps two—where the current ran swiftest. The poles were lashed together with short lengths of cedar bark rope and the whole line braced by heavy props slanting downstream, over which a walkway of other poles was laid.

With a small canoe anchored in a backwash in which to throw the catch, the Indian weir tender walked the poles, using a dip net made by the women out of nettle fibers on the end of a ten-foot pole. The net was strung on a three- or four-foot hoop and a line was attached at one point so the mesh bag could be closed once a fish was caught. Where permanent weirs were not built, short nets were staked out from shore and drawn in.

When rivers were low or for other reasons the salmon stayed in the pools, the Indian fishermen would climb out on rocky ledges and spear the slowly swimming fish. The most effective spears were two- and three-pronged. When three were used the spear was thrust so that the center one pierced the fish, the other two being forced out to close over it, barbs holding it tight.

Some salmon were taken by hook and line from canoes but this method was reserved mainly for halibut and cod. Hooks were fashioned of sharply angled hemlock root or yew wood bound to a shank of bone. Several were attached to a slender rod, four or five feet long, from which the main fishing line extended. The springy arms of the hooks spread to admit the halibut's nose and when he took the bait, helped hold it into the barb. Carved wooden clubs were used to dispatch the fish.

A black cod lure, called quak-ha-pa by the Squamish, resembled an oversize shuttlecock. It was a large, egg-shaped float, from which four or five flukes protruded, bound to the center by wild cherry bark, ends painted red. The fisherman tucked the quak-ha-pa in the tines of a forked spear ten or twelve feet long, pushed it down in the waters as far as he could reach and shook it loose. It floated up, turning over and over. Sometimes the cod bit at it and when it was close to the surface, the Indian jabbed his spear.

Some of the sturgeon caught during the spawning season in the Fraser and and Squamish Rivers weighed as much as six hundred pounds. To catch them a large bone hook was fitted to the end of a ten-foot pole and a line was attached to it to hold it on the pole when the fish was pulled in. Once the sturgeon was hooked, a drag stone was dropped to anchor the canoe or slow it down and after the fish had tired, the stone was heaved up, canoe beached and the sturgeon landed.

Another method was to use long-handled harpoons with detachable heads, floats attached. When one head was embedded in the fish, the float marked its position and further harpoon thrusts could be made until there were enough lines floating to pull in the heavy weight. When made of kelp, dried and treated, the lines could be made of single strands as long as a hundred and fifty feet and were of great strength.

The big schools of herring and smelt were depleted by means of rakes—long, slender sticks in which strips of bone were set to act as teeth. The rakes were handled from canoes paddled into the schools, swept up under the millions of small fish. Where candle fish, or eulachon, abounded in the waters north of the Fraser River,

PROVINCIAL ARCHIVES, VICTORIA

Cowichan Village

they were scooped up in loosely woven baskets. The oil was extracted to use with other foods and was a tribal industry with the Tsimshian and Kwakiutl.

The great masses of eggs released by herring into salty bays drifted shore-ward and clung to the weeds and grasses. Women of the more northern tribes set out in small canoes to gather the glutinous clusters, whisking them off with fir branches and shaking them into woven baskets. Herring spawn was considered a delicacy and relished with dried salmon and other foods. The women also collected bottom growths, both animal and vegetable. The octopus, with its breeding grounds in the San Juan group of islands, populated the shallow waters and was another seasonal tidbit. The tentacles were chopped into short sections and boiled by the hot stone method. When the flesh turned reddish, the skin was stripped off and meat returned to the boiling water, the soft mass scooped into the mouth with clam shells.

The beaches of the inlets and sounds north and south of the Fraser River were well populated with clams. The Indians dug a dozen varieties, using simple wooden slats. Steamed between layers of seaweed laid over beach fires, the clams were skewered and hung on racks to dry, then stored for winter. Crabs, abalones, mussels and barnacles were taken wherever available, shells used for everything from harpoon heads and arrow tips to eating aids. Crabs were netted, small shellfish pried off the rocks. The sea was life itself.

13

PROVINCIAL ARCHIVES, VICTORIA

Musqueam Village—Fraser River

Fight For Survival

Skokomish Chief's Daughter

EDWARD L. CURTIS PHOTO COURTESY
CHARLES E. LAURIAT CO.   UNIVERSITY OF WASHINGTON

PROVINCIAL ARCHIVES, VICTORIA

Cowichan Salmon Weir

Sanetch Village near Esquimault

16

PROVINCIAL ARCHIVES, VICTORIA

Squamish Graves—Fraser River

CITY ARCHIVES, VANCOUVER

PROVINCIAL ARCHIVES, VICTORIA

Making Birch Bark Canoe—Sardis

PROVINCIAL ARCHIVES, VICTORIA

Salish Grave

"Not by Bread Alone"

To have a strong personal power derived from a familiar spirit was the driving urge within every member of the various Coast Salish tribes. This was generally true with most Northwest Coast Indians but the Salish had definite principles and standards of behavior to bring about this spirit power.

To them, a person had two souls—one which lived in his body and stayed close to it or the place where the body had lived, the other departing to high or low regions according to the sort of life the person had lived. Neither of these regions seemed to be a "heaven" or "hell" but rather a mythical place where the weather was perfect, the food good and unlimited.

The everyday life of the Salish involved constant attention to the spirit forces—those of every fish and animal, every tree and rock, every wind and cloud. To live amicably with these spirits meant cultivating their friendship and there were regular procedures to achieve this. If a woman was going clam digging or a man off to hunt deer, each made proper acknowledgments to the clam and deer spirits. The fact that the clam and deer were about to be killed and eaten did not alter the need of spirit cooperation. This seemed to be justified by the fact that food was the greatest necessity of all.

Salmon Cache—Esquimault

CITY ARCHIVES, VANCOUVER

Every Salish child, especially boy, was trained to seek spirit power. At an early age he would be sent out into the woods alone, close to some lake where spirits liked to congregate, and look for the vision which would reveal his personal power, such as hunting power or carving power. He was also trained to accept his revelation modestly, to keep it a secret until the next winter dance or potlatch.

However simplified the life of the Coast Salish, there was plenty of challenge, many ways to improve day-to-day living. They caught more fish, killed more seals, had warmer and stronger clothes, by inventing better tools, implements and weapons. All of these were made from vegetable fibers and shells, the hides, horns, teeth and sinews of animals.

Harpoons were improved by using detachable heads which allowed more than one thrust at a seal or sea otter with the same haft. Heads were made of mussel shell, the blade sharpened and set between two barbs of bone or horn. The haft fitted loosely into a socket between the two barbs, was held sufficiently tight by looping around it the line running from head to float, this line made of braided sinew or kelp. When the sea hunter made his harpoon thrust, he jerked the haft out of the socket and attached another head for another blow.

There were also many ingeniously contrived fish spears used by the Salish tribes. One type utilized several prongs—the center one piercing the fish, the outer ones being thus thrust open and then closing tight over the body of the fish.

Bows and arrows were relied upon for most land hunting, bows rarely over three feet long and made of yew, dogwood, willow and even cedar with their hafts strengthened by winding them with sinew, cherry bark and snake skin. Arrows were slate-tipped for larger game and thin bone points used for ducks, many of these with multiple barbs. Wooden knobs were used for bird arrows.

Since the Coast Salish had little sense of warfare, they spent little time making man-killing weapons, relying upon simple clubs, spears and daggers. Bone and hardwoods were used for spearheads and clubs were carved out of hardwood, being about two and a half feet long. Occasionally a tribe would use clubs with pieces of stone inserted in wooden handles.

Common work implements were confined to stone—the hammer, chisel and adze. The former was not fitted with a handle but shaped to the hand, fingers gripping it and striking it against the wedge-like chisel of nephryte or basalt. All trees were felled, canoes hollowed out and shaped, house timbers cut and smoothed with these three elementary tools.

Salish women had bone and wood knives to split fish, open clams and oysters, separate the fibers of grass and roots. For digging roots and prying shellfish off rocks, they used simple sticks. Thin and strong wooden "paddles" were used for removing cedar bark from trees, beating the fibers and preparing them for weaving.

PROVINCIAL ARCHIVES, VICTORIA

Painted Carvings—Comox

UNIVERSITY OF WASHINGTON

Fish Was Staff of Life

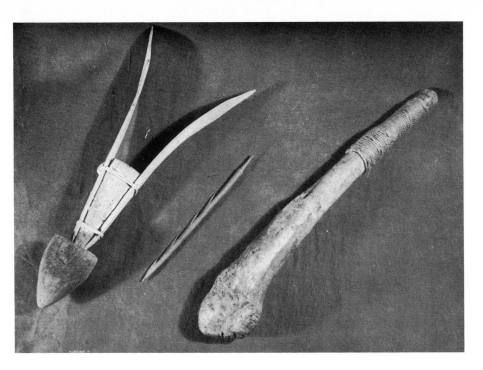

Salish Fish Lure, Spearhead and Club

Salish Fish Spearhead

Salish Stone Implement

PROVINCIAL ARCHIVES, VICTORIA

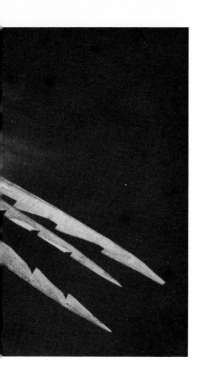
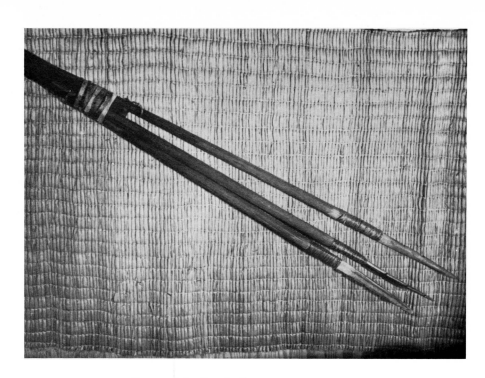

Squamish Duck Spear

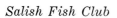

Salish Fish Club   *Squamish Wood-Carving Tools*

Women of Coast Salish Tribes

UNIVERSITY OF WASHINGTON

CITY ARCHIVES, VANCOUVER

Sooke Salmon Cache

EDWARD L. CURTIS PHOTOS COURTESY
CHARLES E. LAURIAT CO.

Summer Mat House　　　*Skokomish Fishing Camp*

Clallam Woman　　　*Makah Woman*

WASH. STATE HISTORICAL SOCIETY　　　UNIVERSITY OF WASHINGTON

Cowichan Tule Gatherer

Lummi Woman

Quilcene Boy

By Spear and Arrow

THE fog held the night back. It was flannel-thick where the river spread itself into a dozen fingers through the tide flats. High over the mainland, light from the east edged over the mountains, exploring the saturated air but not penetrating it.

From far over the islands came the flat morning cries of a thousand northern geese restlessly riding the swells that rolled in with the tide from the open sea. One or two lifted themselves with heavy wings and settled back. A swan circled over them with cumbersome grace, its long neck stretched in curious contemplation of food, flapping ponderously back to a rocky bay.

In a cove to the north where one of the river channels met the sea, a flock of ducks milled lazily as it was joined by others wading out from the frosty grass of the tule flat where they had been feeding. One pair dove into the shallows and, slapping their tails, skittered up off the water into the fog.

They flew low, blindly as far as their sight served them, banking out over the open water and the chorus of geese. Then they sought the lighter air higher up and cruised a mile or more until the first strong rays of the sun pierced the grayness. Curving back in perfect unison, alternately planing and whipping their strong wings in faster flight, they passed over a wooded knob of land and dropped low again. Twice they sounded flight calls, the second time when one sighted the strange colored spot of light below.

It flickered in the quickening breeze coming in with the tide. Both ducks checked their flight and swooped lower. Directly above the glow their wings flattened against the air and brought them into a sharp turn a few feet above the flame. The male, closer to the shore, saw a movement but could not twist away. The next moment it was helplessly fluttering, its neck held fast and body suspended. As its breath ebbed the whush of the female's wings sounded loud and then was stifled by the thick cover of fog.

*　*　*　*　*

The Indian lowered the seven-foot pole and pulled the duck's neck from between the three jagged splints extending from the end, bound tight to it with wild cherry bark. He whacked the bird's head against the gunwale of the canoe and admired the bright colors of the feathers before tossing the warm body on a dozen others. Then he extinguished the pitch blaze in the wad of mud on the covered bow.

Thunderbird and Legendary Ogress

PROVINCIAL ARCHIVES, VICTORIA

The Kwakiutl tribe occupied the mainland coast from Bute Inlet north to Douglas Channel and the northeast coast of Vancouver Island from Johnstone Strait to Quatsino Sound. The mainland area was bisected by Bella Coola territory.

He and his son had been hunting for two hours and were satisfied with their catch. The father was sure his hunting spirit was helping him and he was pleased with his quick and skillful handling of the spear. Now they would go home and sleep some more and since he was sure there would be plenty of ducks and that they would be flying with the colder weather, he would fix nets and get many more when it got dark again.

Geese, ducks and swans found the salt marshes and tideflats rich in food and the great flocks of them were little depleted by Indian forays such as this—and a thousand others. Their flesh was not a staple food item, rather a delicacy, and the tribesmen hunted and caught them only when they were tired of fish. Their usual method of catching them was by use of nets strung on high poles and set up in flyways. The net frames were delicately balanced to fall inward when the ducks struck the net which then held them firmly enmeshed.

Torches or pitch fires on canoes were used when the birds were holding to the water. Two men would lure them into coves or paddle swiftly but silently upon flocks in the tall reeds, throwing spears with sliver-like barbs. Kwakiutl and Nootka hunters caught diving ducks with baited traps under water.

Sea animals were a more important food for all the Northwest Coast tribes. Whales were hunted by those living on the open seas, like the Nootka and Makah. The Haida tribe was an exception. They were seafarers but left the pursuit of such big game to those who made it a highly specialized profession, and to where it was well knitted into tribal tradition.

However, whenever a whale became stranded on the beach, killed by the small killer whales which pursued the slow monsters and tore their flesh, any of the tribes considered it an act of some provider spirit and fell to the feast.

The village closest to the beach where the whale had been washed up would claim the carcass, the people attacking it furiously regardless of the state of the meat, usually bad. The bones were highly prized for tool handles, clubs and weapons.

Hair seals, sea lions and porpoises played off shore all along the Northwest Coast and became a staple item in the Indian diet. Hunting them took rare skill and was restricted by some tribes to the chiefs. Kwakiutl and Nootka ritual gave hereditary rights to seals taken in their waters. Sea otters had an even higher place in Kwakiutl economy as their fur was used extensively for royal ceremonial robes. These large mammals lived in the surface waters and slept as they floated, usually in herds. If the Kwakiutl hunters could surprise them in this helpless state, they killed them with clubs and spears. But if the sea otters came awake, they burst into speedy flight and the canoes were forced into pursuit, perhaps for several miles. If the paddlers outlasted them, the hunters sent sprays of arrows at the animal's heads. Their bows were strong and the arrow points barbed with light lines attached. Once embedded, the points pulled off the arrow shafts and the trailing lines, feather-tipped, allowed the men to follow the quarry.

The hair seal was by far the most dependable source of oil and meat, the skins and stomachs used for storing the oil and for whale hunting floats. Like sea lions, they came out of the sea to rest on the rocks, warm themselves in the sun and rid their hides of lice. It was no great feat to surprise such herds and slaughter hundreds of the slow-moving animals. Nor was it difficult to catch them the way the Haida braves did, with nets stretched between rocks to trap them ashore, or as the

PROVINCIAL ARCHIVES, VICTORIA

Kwakiutl Village—Salmon River

Nootkas, who choked such channels with split logs from which jagged prongs extended.

It was, however, a fine art to hunt them in the open sea as the tribesmen were most often forced to do. Their canoes were especially built for the chase—sleek and fast, the hulls scraped and polished with dried skins. The Indians of the Northern California and Oregon coast waters used harpoons with points set in sockets at the end of heavy shafts. Lines extending from the points were wrapped around the shafts and when the weapons were thrown, the shafts became detached, the seals forced to swim against the trailing drag. They also had harpoons with barbed heads set on several prongs. When the head was set in the seal, the line from it held by one of the canoe men, it was paid out as the seal swam away, then worked in as a man would handle a fish on a hand line.

Kwakiutl, Nootka and Salish sea hunters had differing methods of throwing harpoons which gave them better control and made them more skillful hunters. They also attached small seal-bladder floats to prevent the seal from submerging too far and for tiring him more quickly.

The land hunting preserves of all the Northwest Coast tribes produced an abundance of food and skins. There were deer in the high and low lands to be caught in snares and pitfalls set with sharpened stakes. The men along the Trinidad and Klamath Rivers wore stuffed deer heads complete with horns when stalking the live ones. They were always on the prowl for the albino deer for ceremonial dances, the head and hide of great value. The Nootka stalked deer and elk and trapped them in pits but relied mainly on the winter drive in which the men of whole villages took part. When the animals descended from the deep snow of the mountains, they were walled into some narrow defile or cleft in the rocks.

They used dogs to some extent but it was the Salish people who raised dogs especially for tracking forest animals and herding them into rivers and lakes where they could be killed with bow and arrow or speared from canoes.

Dogs were useful also in driving mountain goat into killing range. This animal grew valuable wool which was roughly woven into blankets such as the Chilkat type with its designs of spirit figures. The black goat horns were made into eating utensils and working tools. The dogs would work the goats down the mountain sides into rocky bottoms or box canyons where spears and arrows could reach them. Such hunting grounds might be held by aggressive chiefs exclusively for family use.

The Kwakiutl did not use dogs but took mountain goat with snares—simple willow branches looped around a sturdy tree which caught the goat's head as he followed a trail. They considered goat meat a rare delicacy—eating the skin as well —steaming it in earthen pits.

Bear, marten, mink, beaver and raccoon were all taken by deadfall traps. A log was set on end at about 45 degree angle, the top resting on a baited trigger. The nibbling animal tripped the bone stake and was killed or pinned to the ground by the falling log. Marmot skins were as valuable as sea otter, a hundred sewed together with nettle fibers to make a robe.

The Haida Indians in the Queen Charlotte Islands took little interest in land hunting since they had so much from the sea. They did want bear skins and when the black beasts came down to fish the rivers in the fall, they set traps and dug pits for as many pelts as they needed for the winter. Bella Coola men likewise, although living in a wonder world of big and small fur bearers, killed only enough black and grizzly bear, marten, wolverine and lynx as they needed for hides. They ate beaver, deer and mountain goat meat, smoking the latter and weaving the wool.

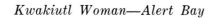
Kwakiutl Women and Children—Quatsino Sound

Kwakiutl Woman—Alert Bay

Kwakiutl Man—Knight Inlet

AL ARCHIVES, VICTORIA

Supports for Kwakiutl House

Village Gathering—Knight Inlet

Kwakiutl Grave Painting—Alert Bay

PROVINCIAL ARCHIVES, VICTORIA

PROVINCIAL ARCHIVES, VICTORIA

House Post—Alert Bay Village

The Kwakiutl people, in physical appearance, were of the general coastal type—heavy and powerful bodies with less well-developed legs. Their faces were broad with cheek bones prominent, eyes brown, hair black and straight with very little of it on face and body. The nose was high, prominent and very frequently hooked.

Both sexes wore the hair long, that of the woman braided in two plaits, the men gathering theirs at the back and tying it in knots. To protect the skin against weather, it was liberally greased, oiled and decorated with painted designs according to the person's nature. When used alone, red denoted aggressiveness or joy;

black, sorrow or despair; but when used together no meaning was read into the designs.

There was little tattooing. Head shaping was achieved by wrapping the infant's head tightly in bands of hide, removing them after some eighteen months and massaging the soft bones. The effect was a flattened forehead and upper cranium and when adults showed such head formation they attained certain dignity and class distinction.

Arm rings, wristlets and ankle bands were worn on occasions of potlatch and winter ceremonials, fashioned of cedar bark and with the rich, mountain goat horn

Grave of Chief Walkus—Alert Bay   *House Front and Post*

which was split and steamed into shape. Bands around the knees were sometimes decorated with deer hoofs and the septum of the nose was pierced for pendants of abalone shell. Dentalium or tooth shell was highly prized all along the Coast, to be hung in strings from ears or hair.

Young Kwakiutl people were expected to bathe every day in fresh water to remove the human smell and make their bodies acceptable to the spirits. Adults who had already acquired personal spirits bathed in **the sea, and this very vigorously, when some spiritual**

benefaction was wanted. Urine was kept in storage and used to wash off the grease and it in turn was removed by fresh water. The crushed bulb of the giant kelp was used as a form of soap. Before ceremonials the women combed their hair often and replaited their braids. After rubbing faces with soft cedar bark, they applied a dressing of deer tallow which was partially removed with coarser cedar bark. Then the face was painted, eyebrows touched up and special lines added to the cheeks.

Alert Bay Village, Kwakiutl

Alert Bay House Post

Interior Kwakiutl House

PROVINCIAL ARCHIVES, VICTORIA

Kwakiutl Trading Party

EDWARD L. CURTIS PHOTO COURTESY
CHARLES E. LAURIAT CO.

When the Chief Took a Wife

To a tribe whose every movement was governed by the wishes of animal and bird spirits, a Kwakiutl royal marriage ceremony was a gala affair. And if the bride was of a different tribe it was a lavish show of pomp and pride.

A chief's family was necessarily wealthy and no cost was spared to impress the foreign tribesmen with his importance. Months were spent on the fashioning of masks, costumes, bird and animal images and in repainting canoes and preparing food. And when the groom sallied forth to meet the bride, who might well have been a total stranger to him, known only by the fact that she was the daughter of a powerful chief, he became second in importance to the theatrics of the occasion.

The photograph below shows him standing quietly and inconspicuously in the stern of the canoe while the man inside the Thunderbird holds the center of the stage, flapping his wings and screeching in imitation of the great benefactor. The view at the right shows the Wasp, Thunderbird and Grizzly bear—three of the Kwakiutl dieties who are here carrying their good wishes to the wedding.

On the next pages the chief and his new wife, richly and royally clad, stand on the "bride's seat" in the stern while a member of the groom's family dances in the bow, accompanied by song and paddle-thumping.

The carved and painted figureheads of this canoe represents the Eagle, bird highly sacred to the Kwakiutl. Those on the canoes on preceding pages depict the Whale, Frog and Sisiutl, mythical two-headed serpent. The sails shown were of cedar bark matting and used usually only on long voyages and for state ceremonies.

Masked Dancers in Wedding Party

Kwakiutl Groom Comes for Bride

EDWARD L. CURTIS PHOTOS COURTESY
CHARLES E. LAURIAT CO.

EDWARD L. CURTIS PHOTO COURTESY
CHARLES E. LAURIAT CO.

Kwakiutl Wedding Party

Dance to Bring Back Moon

THERE was no logical reason for a moon to go straying off in the sky. One minute it was there, round and full, and then it was slowly disappearing—swallowed by some unknown and unseen creature. This was the Kwakiutl belief when the moon went into an eclipse and the people had to get busy right away and bring it back.

A new fire was built on the highest place back of the village and everybody gathered up all the old clothing, dirty mats, refuse and hair they could find. They piled it on the flames until the smudge covered the whole area and the stench rose with the billows of smoke. The people danced in and out of the fumes, sending their appeals into the high places. They knew that when the wicked creature sneezed and choked on the smoke, it would disgorge the moon and things would be normal.

Most Kwakiutl dances were performed in the winter and were the expressed rights of the various secret societies, each member's ancestors having obtained dance and song privileges from the supernatural beings who controlled them. During the season when food was stored and there was very little work to do, the ceremonies and dances began, as performed by such legendary societies as the Hamatsa or Cannibal group, the Grizzly Bear, Hamshamtses, Crazy Man or Warrior societies. On these occasions the nobles left off their own name and clan affiliations, assumed their secret society appellations.

The main purpose of the winter ceremonials was to initiate the chiefs' sons or nobles-to-be into the order. This rite began with the initiate secluding himself in the woods for a number of days to become blessed with the spirit which ruled the society. When he returned, he became the center of the show, which was an enactment of the first historical one in which the ancestor encountered the original supernatural being. The fact that it was play in no way detracted from the players' enthusiasm and realistic performances. With masks, fantastic costumes, rattles, whistles and weird noises, the dancers attempted to make the uninitiated believe they were dealing with real spirits.

There was often savage violence in the dances to awe the audience and lift the society in the eyes of members of rival ones. Should a member make a false dance step, the other dancers pretended to attack and murder him, sometimes with disastrous results.

One of the dances of the Cannibal Society, the dlugwola or "find a supernatural treasure," is described in British Columbia Heritage Series, Volume 7.

> The performance of this dance is an announcement of one's intention to become a "Cannibal" later on. (This was not meant literally but referred to the later acquisition of a "Cannibal" dance.) Only high-ranking youths may use it. The being inspiring the novice is "One-making-war-all-around-the-world." When the whistles of this spirit are heard inspiring the novice, all the initiates are called to sing for him. This assemblage is called *yexa*, from an exclamation used when something is lost or vanishes. In the midst of his dance, the voice of the spirit is heard again, and as the dancer disappears the people shout "ye!" For four days the dancer remains hidden, cared for by someone who has had the same dance. According to the fiction of the

EDWARD L. CURTIS PHOTO COURTESY
CHARLES E. LAURIAT CO.

Dance to Bring Back Moon

rite, he is supposed to be transported around the world by his spirit during this time. On the fourth day the whistles sound, signalling the return of the dancer. He shows himself on the beach across from the village. The master of ceremonies and a Healing Dancer are sent to see who this being may be. (In the case of several dancers having disappeared, they all "come down" at the same time.) When the master of ceremonies returns to announce the identity of the dancer, a raft is constructed and certain men go to capture him. He dances holding his arms extended forward, fists clenched, and thumbs sticking up, instead of using the split-stick rattles of other dancers. On the fourth night he displays the lance from "One-making-war-all-around-the-world." He is brought in standing in a canoe, holding his lance, from which a row of carved heads are suspended. He may also have masks to show. Afterwards he is purified by the "Healers."

The opening scene of each drama always developed along the same lines, no matter what society was giving the performance. The chief actor was always a novice who had been carried away to the upper regions by the principal supernatural being of the society concerned. In the Cannibal Society dance, the novice, on his return, being obsessed by his recent experience, no longer behaved in a human manner. Instead he dashed about like a wild thing biting at people, for he had acquired an appetite for human flesh. He stared blankly, even at his own parents, and nervously avoiding the touch of the people who sought to lay hold on him. He could not be caught, and with all their efforts the people were unable to bring a sign of recognition into his face. They, therefore, sought to charm him back to human life by songs and dances, some of which were performed by a woman, *Ki'nqalalala,* who danced in front of the novice offering in her arms what was supposed to be a human corpse. This attracted the obsessed "cannibal," and he followed her in the d a n c e as she walked backward four times around the fire.

In the first dance of this performance the novice was so wild that he wore no clothes, and danced around the fire in a squatting position, advancing in long leaps with both feet together, his arms extended sideways, and his hands trembling. At

47

EDWARD L. CURTIS PHOTOS COURTESY
CHARLES E. LAURIAT CO.

Types of Kwakiutl Men

Kwakiutl of Quatsino Sound

the end of the fourth turn about the fire, the novice disappeared. In the second dance the novice emerged from his room at the back of the house, and was again attracted by the woman holding the corpse. By this time he was becoming more conscious of his human nature and had donned a blanket. At first he advanced in the same position as before, but he gradually straightened himself, and as he took each step he drew one knee up almost to his chest and lowered himself slightly by partially bending the other. Again four turns were taken around the fire before the novice returned to his room.

The other acts were staged in the same manner, but in these the dancer stood upright, and in one of the acts the woman, as she came to an upturned drum, made motions toward it as though to place the corpse upon it.

The woman was not the only power brought to tame the novice. Throughout all the acts appropriate songs were sung to a rhythm produced by the beating of batons on boards. This was done with periodic changes in musical pitch, in tempo, and in volume. In moments of ecstasy the music became so rapid and loud that the voices of the singers could scarcely be heard. There were many side effects and variations on the central theme. In some of them it was common for several older persons, whose initiations had taken place in former years, to join in.

Membership in the secret societies was more or less fixed. Hence, when a chief brought his heir into a society and bestowed on him his names and privileges, that chief dropped his membership and became again an outsider, although one with a special name denoting his former connections.

EDWARD L. CURTIS PHOTOS COURTESY
CHARLES E. LAURIAT CO.

Using Fire Drill—Koskimo

Inland Kwakiutl—Kingcombe River

Kwakiutl in Winter Dress

EDWARD L. CURTIS PHOTO COURTESY
CHARLES E. LAURIAT CO.

52

Masked Dancers in Winter Ceremony

Kwakiutl Woman Gathering Abalone

EDWARD L. CURTIS PHOTO COURTESY
CHARLES E. LAURIAT CO.

South for Plunder

THE cold weather was here, the Haida chief at Skidans reflected, and it was the best time to take the voyage south. Most people did not like stormy weather and waited until the winds grew weaker and the air warmer. No, he was not like that. He would travel when the wind blew hard and waves tried to upset the canoes. This was the best time because nobody expected visitors. And he did not want to be expected. What he wanted was slaves and other trade goods.

He would visit the Kwakiutl on the big island to the south where the sea ran swift in the narrow channel. He would find people asleep in one certain village early in the morning. He would take only twenty men with him in two canoes, half of them slaves. There would be one spirit doctor who would do no work but transfer his power to the souls of the people on shore, to make them die more quickly. He did not like to kill people to get more slaves and trade goods but if he had to kill them, he would rather they be Kwakiutl. They were never very friendly and usually had many sea otter skins. These were very valuable for trading with the Skeena River people.

There was one problem. Word had come to him that a Kwakiutl chief from the mainland to the east was making a visit at the Haida village of Ksodze. This chief had said he needed more slaves to prove how rich he was. Very well, he would bring this Kwakiutl chief some slaves—the ones he captured on this voyage—and he would get eulachon oil.

Yet it would not be well to let this Kwakiutl man know that the slaves had come from another Kwakiutl territory. It was better not to disturb friendly relations. So on this voyage all the Kwakiutl would be killed and nobody would know who killed them. Only the slaves, who would be of other tribes, would be taken alive. And nobody listened to the tales slaves told.

This trip, the chief concluded, would be his alone and only he would be praised for it when he returned with heavily laden canoes. He did not want anybody, except his own family and a few trusted men, to know he was going. Most of all he did not want Lukstch, the chief in the next village, to know. Lukstch would try to delay the expedition while he got ready one of his own. Lukstch was always enraged when some other chief got the better of him in war or gambling or trading. He was a bad enemy even though he was a Haida and a good sea hunter.

The habitat of the Haida was limited to all of the Queen Charlotte Islands and the southern fingers of Prince of Wales Island.

With his plans made, the chief spoke quietly to the men who would go with him. He said nothing to the slaves but he knew they would quickly see a voyage was coming soon because of all the preparations. He would let his son take charge of the slaves and if any made talk, have them held under water until they swallowed it. So he called his son, son-in-law and other men into council.

First he distributed the medicine the spirit doctor said would give everybody power and strength on the voyage. "You will eat no fish and meat or drink any water until the day before we leave," he told them. "Instead you will eat fern roots and wild lily bulbs and berry cake and the women will make some salal berry mush with eulachon oil. When we start on the voyage we can chew dried salmon and anything else we want to take. Now—turn the canoes over and burn the bottoms clean."

Each voyager's wife was told to make two belts from whale sinew and to paint on them designs to represent the spirits of the slaves who were to be captured. Each man and wife were to wear these day and night until the trip south began and the return home had been made. The day before the canoes set out they would exchange each other's belts.

Spears were repaired, new bows, arrows and clubs made. Sealskin floats were attached to cedar bark lines, these to be secured to the new slaves who might try to drown themselves. New paddles were shaped, new baskets woven and filled with provisions.

The women were carefully instructed as to how they should sleep while their husbands were away. All would occupy one house by themselves, guarding each other's conduct, eating sparingly, scrubbing their bodies every day to have them clean for new tattooing when the men returned. During the nights the canoes were traveling to the place of attack, they must lie with their heads in that direction. When the moon came full, the time for the start of the return journey, they would reverse their bodies, heads pointed to the north.

Now came the day of departure. The ten slaves carried the thirty-foot canoe into the surf and held it over the water until the spirit man had climbed in. He traveled lightly but still had a basket full of soul catchers and rattles. Then the chief marched solemnly down the beach. Once he was seated in the bow of the other canoe, which was newly decorated with the design of a sea monster devouring a fish, the five warriors filed along the left side of each boat, all ten holding their paddles stiffly in front of them. Then the slaves pushed the canoes out and took the paddles.

All this was accomplished in absolute silence, the women out of sight in their lodge. When the canoes were seen meeting the high waters beyond the land promontory, they emerged and quietly built a fire in the secluded place the chief had pointed out. When they looked seaward again they could see their men and the slaves paddling in a steady rhythm. They put more wood on the fire and vowed to keep it blazing until the canoes returned with perhaps a third one filled with riches and prizes of the voyage.

Such ventures as this were common experiences with Haida chiefs. They were keen and expert traders and to get trade goods they let their aggressive natures carry them into raids upon other tribes. They were not naturally warlike but possessed, in fact, an innate desire for harmonious relations. Yet avarice was stronger. They were courageous but prudent and like all other Northwest Coastal Indians seldom took chances against an enemy of superior numbers. The small raiding party, in a surprise attack on a village, was the better part of valor.

The Haidas made property raids by canoe as far south as Puget Sound on the Clallam, Nisqually and other tribes but more frequently on the Kwakiutl and Cowichan people of eastern Vancouver Island. Nor did they hesitate to spring upon unsuspecting villages in their own Queen Charlotte and Prince of Wales Islands. Many of these raids were part of continual feuds carried on with their neighbors or in revenge for some hurt to family pride. After a slaying or injury, the relative of the victim attempted to retaliate but it was material indemnity, not blood, he wanted in payment. He did not always get it, however, and often these feuds lasted for several years, finally determined by savage warfare which completely wiped out either one village or the other.

One custom of the Northern tribes was to strike out and wantonly kill one or more persons when a chief died. Even though his death was from natural causes, his relatives wished to send others with him to his final resting place and to spread the mourning over villages. Death was inflicted ruthlessly on the first people the warriors saw, even on people of their own village if they happened to be seen first.

The Haidas practised scalping and cut off their victims' heads as trophies of victory to display on poles in front of their houses. Custom decreed also that such enemy heads be mounted on the upright paddles of any warriors slain in battle. Similar tactics were followed by Tlingit and Nootka tribesmen who took the heads of the victims and removed the scalps as they traveled homeward.

The Kwakiutl had no hereditary impulses to battle. They were also too busy gathering food supplies in the good traveling weather, and indulging in ceremonials in the winter, to spend time preparing for fights. They made war only when driven to it by some offense against their tribal or personal honor.

The sister of a Kwakiutl chief and her daughter, says a tribal tale, were lost out of a canoe returning home from a visit to foreign parts. The chief knew the small canoe might have been swamped in the heavy seas but he was determined to place the blame on Indians in whose territory the drownings occurred—the Sanetch tribe. He called a meeting of the village men, drove a short post in the earthen floor of his house and the warriors pledged themselves to avenge the deaths by placing hemlock wreaths on the pole.

All the wives would stay home and rub their bodies with hemlock twigs. They made kelp garlands into the bulbs of which the men had blown their breath. The men wore them for a day and then the women hung them high up and kept them well guarded. If the bulbs of air were broken, the men would die. The common men agreed to do all work necessary including the canoe paddling while the women gathered tules and mussels.

Preparing for the raid, the warriors built a fire and charred the canoe bottoms. Retiring to the woods, they rubbed their naked bodies with hemlock branches. Late at night they bathed with their wives in the river and went home to sleep on separate mats. At dawn they moored the canoes in deep water.

When all the men were ready to leave, they wore the kelp garlands in which their breath had been captured. A drum began to sound on shore and the wives appeared wearing special belts, faces blackened. On the beach they took the kelp garlands thrown by their husbands and ran back to the communal lodge to hang them until the men returned.   Then all was silence as the canoes were manned and departed.

The raid was a success and accomplished with no loss of blood on the part of the attackers.   They swooped down on the first Sanetch house they came to, found seven people sleeping.   They threw a large bark mat over them so they could not escape and six were killed.   The seventh, a young girl, was taken back as a slave.

Warfare was secondary also to the Bella Coola tribe but necessary for defense. They were not of militant natures and lacked central authority, having no power-wielding chiefs.   They preferred a potlatch anytime to a war party.   They did have a great abundance of food resources which removed the necessity of fighting for it but which at the same time made them vulnerable to attack from the Kwakiutl who had less food of their own.

Lack of strong leaders was a serious handicap to this highly cultured tribe but, offsetting it, was the comparative safety of the narrow valley in which they lived. The inland Bella Coola villagers were often warned of Kwakiutl raids by those in the outer villages who hurried after the attackers to help repel them.   If one village had been attacked, members of several might gather to discuss retaliation and select a leader by popular choice—usually a man who had given many potlatches and who saw a chance to make his position stronger.   But he was never strong enough to compel anyone to fight except his own slaves. And frequently men who had joined a foray of revenge found the idea not to their liking and simply deserted, returning home for more constructive work.   Peace was precious.

Haida Graves—Masset

PROVINCIAL ARCHIVES, VICTORIA

Sticks and Bones

THE urge to win at games and gain riches the easy way—by gambling—was ever present with the Northwest Coast Indians. A man with a knack for outguessing his opponent and who took the trouble to develop it to a high point could win anything from a basket of salmon eggs to a wife. At any hour of the day or night, two or more men could be found playing slahal or variations of it, especially during the winter when the fishing was not good. And it is presumed they played just as eagerly in the summer when it was good.

At potlaches, wedding celebrations or winter ceremonials the younger men had games of physical skill such as wrestling, foot races, tugs of war and jumping. Whole groups participated and spectators placed bets on the winners. Children had dancing contests which were essentially feats of endurance. They also played a tug of war game for fun, pulling on poles instead of ropes.

On the beaches in summer, when two tribes were having festivities, they might play a form of shinny for slaves, canoes, shell money or blankets. Each side had from ten to twenty players, each wielding two sticks one of which was curved at one end. Goals varied from six to eight hundred feet apart, the game consisting of knocking a wood knot, about the size of a dog's head, across it. The stick in the right hand was for propelling the knot, the other for whatever malicious purpose came suddenly to mind. The game had no referee and few rules. Casualties were high and varied according to the stakes. A man about to lose his last fish spear or a hard-working wife might be justified in whacking off a strange ear. It is conceivable the knot and the main object of the game were sometimes forgotten in an eagerness to eliminate a mortal enemy. Since this was play, he could easily be forgiven.

The Nootkas threw stones at targets and played a game in which one man rode on the back of a runner, opposing players attempting to "unhorse" him. In another of their games two teams, some hundred feet apart, used forked sticks to catch a large hoop thrown in the air. The Kwakiutl Indians along the Kitimat River carried out mock warfare, using bows and arrows with blunt tips. Youths divided their forces into two groups, selected officers who appointed scouts and led the skirmishes.

The various games of chance were simple to play and required little equipment. The games were basic all along the Coast, each tribe adding its own variations and calling them by different names. The play was similar and the end result universal. Some men got rich and their families lived in high estate. Others went poor and often into slavery, their women and children with them.

The popular bone game was called lahal by the Nootkas and slahal by the Salish. Four bones were used—such as the large ones in duck wings. The two representing men were painted white, the two representing women, black. Two leaders sat opposite each other and with each were grouped their followers who kept the play at high pitch by shouts as they beat sticks against heavy boards in a slow but steady rhythm.

Each leader was given a white and black bone. The first leader held one in each hand, the second man guessing which hand held the white one. He did so by slapping his left breast with his left palm and pointing with right forefinger. If the guess was right the winner got both bones and one tally stick.

In that case, the second leader had the four bones and, rattling them together, passed one pair to each of two people at his side. They in turn rattled them and then with a bone in each hand, worked their arms forward and back. The opposing leader made his guess as to where both of the white bones were. If he won the first guess and lost the second, he won one tally and regained one set of bones. If he lost both guesses, he gave up two tallies. In this event the leader with the bones repeated the rattling and passed the bones to two different men. The game went on until either leader lost all his tallies.

The number of these was set before the game, usually from fifty to one hundred. They represented the stakes and all must be lost at least once. They were cedar slivers sharpened at one end and inserted in the ground at the edge of the planks on which the men beat time.

Another gambling game, played by two men only with their supporters clustered around them, was concerned with guessing the black disc out of nine white ones. The two players kneeled facing each other fourteen feet apart, each at the end of his bark mat about one-third unrolled and pinned to the ground by six sticks. The tally sticks were fashioned of hardwood, flattened on one side, rounded on the other, and were planted in a row alongside. Two of them of a different color were placed in the middle of the row, this indicating the halfway point of the game. To win, one player had to gain all the sticks.

The first man wrapped the ten discs in shredded cedar bark, shook the bundle vigorously and tore the bundle apart so there were five discs in each half. He laid both on his mat, circled around them, each of his hands in counterclockwise motion. The second player guessed which bundle hid the black disc by pointing a finger. The first unwrapped this package and rolled the contents on his opponent's mat, scattering the second package on his own. If the guess was wrong, the first player got two tallies—if right, the guesser took the discs, but no tallies. He played and from then on a loser paid only one stick for a wrong guess.

A woman's game, said to be played widely in the Puget Sound region, was called smetali and involved the use of four beaver teeth, two with black lines to represent men, two with black dots for women, one of these having a small strip of skin tied around it. The undersides of all four teeth were unmarked. The winner was required to get forty tally sticks to win. Four were won when a player threw the teeth and the one with the skin on it landed with marks up, the other three marks down, or vice versa. Two tallies were taken when all teeth came marks up or all marks down. One stick was won when both men landed up and women down, or vice versa. Other throws paid nothing.

In contrast to the singing, drumming and excitement when the men gambled, the women's contests drew a limited audience of general disinterest. A possible reason for this is the stakes were low, in keeping with the women's own lack of wealth, and the games were little more than pastimes. Most of the women derived more pleasure out of teaching boys to play simple forms of games their elders played.

Many of these children's games were merely plays on the imagination, inspired by what the young eyes saw of adult life. The boys played at hunting and fishing, the girls at keeping house, picking berries and digging roots. Both naturally liked games which made them laugh. The Kwakiutl children played one in which opposing sides were lined up, each in its turn imitating the antics of certain animals while the other side poked fun at the players to make everyone laugh. The leaders of each side had piles of shells from which they paid forfeits for each one of his or her team who laughed. The shell was placed on the ground and the laugher crawled up to it very slowly. The side paying the forfeit made funny remarks and if one on the other team laughed, the shell was put back in its pile.

The Bella Coola tribe pitted the men of one village against another in spear-throwing contests. The spears were small wooden ones tipped with bone. The teams were made up of five players each, each player having a special name according to his position. He made personal bets with the man in the same position on the opposing team.

A chunk of wood resembling an animal head was set up as a target and the leader of one team threw his spear into the ground as near this object as he could. The opposing leader tried to get his spear closer, and if he failed to do so, his second man threw and each in succession until one spear landed closer than the rival leader's. Then the throwing shifted to this side, each player trying to beat the closer throw. The team of the player who got closest to the target won and each man of the losing team paid his share.

Games such as this might continue all day and all night if the stakes were high enough—and most of the time they were. The games were serious business and men not only entered into them with wilful determination to win but also made ceremonial gestures to the spirits to increase their chances. The expert players who trained and prayed had the profound admiration of the younger set which followed the players from village to village and spurred their favorites to win with frenzied shouts and shrieks. Games were fun, but gambling was the road to riches.

Haida House Posts

PROVINCIAL ARCHIVES, VICTORIA

Haida Crest Poles—Queen Charlottes

Decayed Poles and Houses—Masset

PROVINCIAL ARCHIVES, VICTORIA

Masset—
Queen Charlotte Islands

Haida House—Masset

Haida House Posts

Memorial Poles—Skidegate

PROVINCIAL ARCHIVES, VICTORIA

Haida Weapons Showed Carving Skill

THE Tsimshians and other northern tribes considered Haida canoes the finest built and were willing to trade vast quantities of eulachon oil for them. The wood came from prime Queen Charlotte Island red cedar, the canoes were exceedingly seaworthy the finishing most expert. Haida craftsmen had a superior sense of design and natural aptitude for carving.

These abilities carried over into the shaping of their tools and weapons, showing most clearly in the war clubs, knife and spear handles and seal hunting bows. Their stone axes, mauls and adzes had wooden hafts but, whereas most tribesmen left them plain, the Haidas shaped them for better hand gripping and with artistic gestures toward their personal spirits. War clubs were generally carved from single pieces of yew or hard driftwood. Either end might be carved to represent bird, man or animal and some of the designs became very detailed.

Bone knives were sometimes made with a short blade at one end, long blade at the other and carved handle in between. This allowed the wielder to make a forward thrust, then another in quick reverse. Many of the more elaborately carved weapons were made for ceremonial use rather than for actual fighting, the symbolic designs cut in low relief and made even more striking by red, green and blue paint.

Haida Weapons

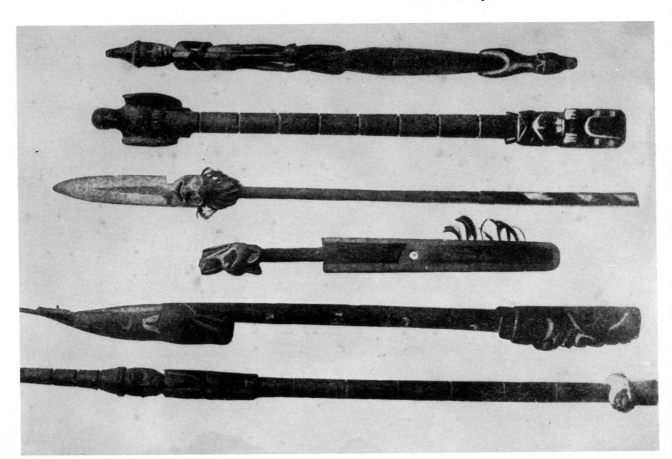

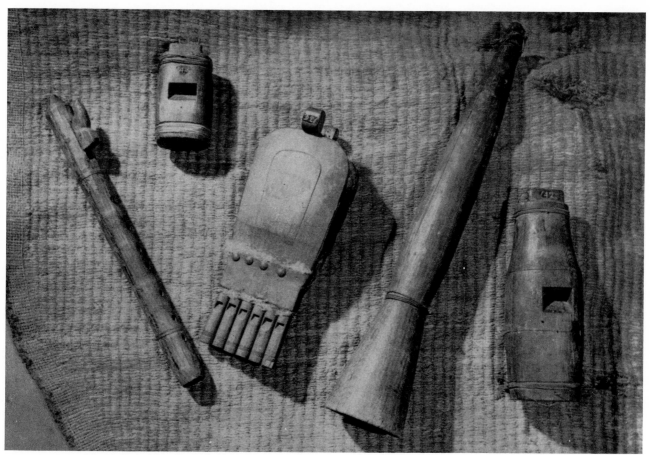

PROVINCIAL ARCHIVES, VICTORIA

Haida Ceremonial Whistles

Haida Baskets—Queen Charlottes

Haida Man—Kung

EDWARD L. CURTIS PHOTOS COURTESY
CHARLES E. LAURIAT CO.

Chief's Tomb—Yan

PROVINCIAL ARCHIVES, VICTORIA

Poles at Kasaan

Haida Woman

PROVINCIAL ARCHIVES, VICTORIA

Haida Village—Skidegate

Haida Chief's Grave—Skidegate

Salmonberry Mash Drying

PROVINCIAL ARCHIVES, VICTORIA

The Canoe was War and Peace

THE high road was the water line. All the Northwest Coast Indians lived on rivers and fiord-like inlets or sandy-beached bays and used canoes far more than they did their legs. The whaling tribes and the bold marauders of the North took to deep water as a natural part of a primitive life.

In almost all this Indian territory there was an endless supply of timber and, since the logs floated, they made a natural means of getting people and goods from one point to another. Cedar was found to be the most practical because it was light in the water, soft enough to be worked handily even with crude implements, strong enough to withstand rough usage, the crushing force of ocean waves and was practically rot proof. Wherever there was an abundance of cedar, there were Indians who became skilled in canoe making, the best ones being produced by the tribes with artistic and decorative urgings. A desire to excel led them to fashion better woodworking tools.

To the Nootkas on their big island sea reach, the canoe was life itself—the means of taking whales and fishing the halibut banks far off the coast. The big Nootka dugout canoe was such an excellently constructed and seaworthy vessel it became a popular type of voyaging craft with other tribes, particularly the groups of Salish in the Gulf of Georgia area. It was featured by a square stern and an upswept "dog face" prow and built in all lengths up to forty and fifty feet.

The falling and rough shaping of cedar trees was usually done during the winter; the steaming, spreading and finishing, a part of the spring labor. The trees were sometimes cut down entirely and all work done on the log as it lay flat on the ground. Often, however, only the big canoe section was removed from the standing tree. The method here was to chisel into the lower trunk perhaps two-thirds of the diameter, then split the tree upwards. Cedar trees taper sharply, are short and chunky rather than tall and stately. In some cases it may have been necessary for one man to climb the tree and cut off the top but it is generally supposed the split went on up through the small branches of the crown.

With the section on the ground, two or three men started work shortening it to overall length and hollowing it out. Obviously this was a long and laborious task. The primitive chisels were made from whale bone or the horns of elk or deer, edges rubbed on rocks until they presented some degree of sharpness, butt ends bound with bone or wooden rings to prevent spreading. Hammers were of hard stone, some-

The Bella Coola people lived on Burke and Dean Channels of the northern mainland between the two Kwakiutl sections.

times pestle-shaped so that the blow was a thrust of fist and arm rather than a swing from the shoulder. A type of adze was made by grinding and polishing mussel shell, for digging out the interior wood and working down the outside. When the hull was shaped, it was smoothed by more chipping and scraping, then finished still smoother by vigorous rubbing with sand and matting. The outside was scorched with hot stones to prevent it from cracking in the hot sun, then the prow and stern pieces were added. Depending on the length, three or four men would require three weeks to three months to complete a canoe.

Nootka paddles were made from yew wood or other hard wood obtained from interior tribes. They ranged between five and six feet in length and were of two types— one shaped like a leaf, the other tapered to a sharp point. The latter was a formidable weapon when the Nootkas were bent on war, the point raked down across an enemy face or used spear-like to gash into his chest.

The tribes of the rigorous northern climates also made canoe building a great skill and gave it spiritual and artistic meaning. With the Kwakiutl on the mainland along Knight and Rivers Inlet and on the northern shore of Vancouver Island, the task was a very serious undertaking, approached with many taboos and continued petitions to the spirits controlling trees and tools. Humbled by much bathing and abstinence from frivolities, a man would face the cedar he was to cut and speak to it. He would determine where he wanted the tree to fall, make a few gashes in the bark and throw a few small chips in that direction. Then he would address the tree again. "O, life giver, now that you have seen the way a small part of your all-powerful being goes, put all of you that way." And every important phase of the canoe project would be directed by such supplications.

The log was rolled so that the part intended for the canoe lay on the bottom side. The unwanted part was then removed by wedges and the hollowing of the hull commenced by fire and finished with adze and chisel work. The shaping was done entirely by eye and as the craft began to take shape, the taboos and prayers increased, mounting to fervent heights when the sides must be spread. By this time the canoe was resting on its keel and it was partially filled with water brought to a boil by hot stones. Old mats were laid across the gunwales to confine the steam. The worker was now in a most contrite mood, earnestly imploring the spirits to hold off any cold wind that might cause the wood to split and allowing no man to help who might in any way offend the spirit guardians. When the wood was soft enough, thwarts were forced in to spread the sides and give the proper beam.

The outside was hardened by fire and by painting it with a mixture of fish oil and ground charcoal. Sails were made of thin cedar strips sewed together and later cedar bark mats were used. Once a canoe had proven its worth, the owner took care of it with great pride. It was always beached stern first or, if possible, carried ashore when waves were high and covered with rough mats to protect it from the sun.

In his book, *The Tlingit Indians*, Aurel Krause, who lived with this tribe in the general area of the Lynn Canal in the 1880s, describes the methods he saw those tribesmen use. "Most striking of all the equipment necessary for the Tlingit in fishing is his canoe, not only on account of its usefulness but also for its artistic construction.

"These canoes are usually made during the winter, the larger and better ones of a red cedar log, the second grade ones of Sitka spruce or of poplar trees. Strong and sound trunks which have not been bent or twisted spirally were sought for this purpose. Felling is still done in this fashion: with an axe a hole is cut on the windward side of the standing tree and a fire set in it which slowly eats its way through until after a number of days the trunk falls over. Then it is first trimmed down with the elbow adze and not until the desired shape is achieved is it hollowed out. To make a wall of even thickness, small holes are bored from the outside and wooden plugs about two or three centimeters stuck in them. When the workman strikes them from within, he knows he has reached the right thickness. In order to make as large a canoe as possible from the given trunk, about two-thirds of its diameter is used, but such a canoe has a very clumsy shape, for the side walls bend inwards at the top and the bow and stern have little height so that the craft is easily overturned in the water. To obtain a more pleasing rounded body with greater stability, the canoe is spread. After the holes mentioned above have been closed with wooden plugs, the canoe is filled with water which is heated by means of dropping in hot stones; then cross pieces are set to spread the softening walls and gradually they are replaced with longer ones until finally an even and efficient shaping of the sides is achieved.

"Canoes are made in varying sizes, the smallest are for only two or three people, the largest carry thirty or more men . . . . . several were forty-five feet long and held about sixty men. Among other things the walls. . . . are extended with side planking. On the larger ones the bow is often ornamented with a carved figure and the side walls are gaily painted. . . . they also had names such as Sun, Moon, Constellations, Earth, Island, Shaman, Whale, Otter, Eagle, Raven and similar ones with the idea carried out in the figures on the bow and stern.

"In shape the canoes were alike, long, narrow and with high pointed bow and stern. Since neither a keel or outriggers were used, it took all the skill a Tlingit had to keep the light craft from capsizing in stormy weather and high waves. In the smaller ones he had to sit on the bottom with his legs stretched out in front of him, or kneel in order to keep the center of gravity as low as possible; but even in the larger ones moving about had to be accomplished with the greatest care. The canoes were propelled with short paddles about one and one-half millimeters (58½") long. These had a crutch handle and were manipulated by one hand pushing the paddle forward, while the other hand, grasping the middle of the paddle, pulled the blade through the water. Similar, somewhat larger blades were used for steering. For celebrations brightly painted paddles were used. . . . . .

"Such a valuable piece of property was handled with care by the Tlingit. In landing they tried to avoid running up on stones or rocks and carried, not dragged, it beyond the reach of the tide. During travel in the sunshine, the sides were kept damp by sprinkling water on them, and when idle on the beach, it was protected from the sun by a cover of woolen blankets or cedar bark matting. If, however, the boat is damaged, as may easily happen with its thin walls, only two or three centimeters thick, the harm is repaired with great care by setting in a new piece of wall and sewing the break with roots of Sitka spruce or yellow cedar or by dovetailing in pieces of wood and making the joints watertight with pitch.

"In spite of the skill with which the Tlingit handle their canoes, they did not like to risk the open sea in stormy weather. If, however, they are overtaken by bad weather during a trip, they show themselves equal to the danger. With keen attention they watch every oncoming wave and if an unusually high one threatens to overturn the canoe, they strike it with flat paddles which gives the impression that they are pushing the sea down, while in reality they push the boat toward the crest of the wave."

The red cedar grew to its finest size and quality in the Queen Charlotte Islands, the home of the Haidas. Relatively free from knots, straight grained and easily worked, the wood made possible canoes that were the envy of other tribes and a large demand for them came from the south. Even the Tsimshians who themselves built good canoes considered the Haidas' product of very great value and were always willing to trade quantities of eulachon oil for them.

Canoes for the Haida raids on southern peoples and for making other journeys were as long as seventy-five feet with a seven-foot beam. Such a craft could carry up to forty persons with perhaps two tons of baggage and trade goods. Their ordinary family canoe measured about twenty-five feet, used mainly for fishing and hunting.

As with the Kwakiutl, the manufacture of a Haida canoe not only required great skill and forethought but the designer, his wife, family and helpers, as well as the man for whom the canoe was being made, were subject to certain restrictions on their daily habits in order that the spirits might be pleased and cooperate in making the work go well and the final result be a perfectly balanced, smoothly operating canoe.

Since they used a canoe with high projecting bow and stern, a sharp vertical cutwater or forefoot and a rounded counter, they gave particular attention to these elements as well as the polishing of the exterior which was done with dried dogfish skin. The canoes of wealthy families were dextrously painted with heraldic designs.

The projecting bow and stern units which served to repel wave crests that might otherwise swamp the craft, were scarffed and fitted to the hull, sewed tight with withes of tough vines and roots threaded through drilled holes.

With the colorful Bella Coola tribesmen on the Burke and Dean Rivers flowing into Queen Charlotte Sound, woodworking was a highly developed accomplishment and this extended to canoe building. Their ocean-going types were similar to the Haidas but they built one for the rivers called a spoon canoe. It ranged from twenty to thirty feet in length and four to five in width, was double-ended without a keel. One man could easily handle the craft in smooth water but a long journey required two or four, each man using a ten-foot pole with spare paddles for use in deep water. Spoon canoes were very stable, an estimable quality in the rapids.

Their canoe used for the ocean was deeper and narrower, with an extension near the stern acting as a keel. It was seaworthy enough to weather any storm. While not ordinarily built in big sizes, one has been described as being forty-five feet in length, three and a half in depth, painted black and decorated with fish designs and sea otter teeth outlined along the gunwales.

The Quinault Indians below Cape Flattery constructed very superior canoes, with high bows and sterns as in the North, many of them carrying fifty and sixty people. They sold and traded them to the less adept woodworkers on the inland waters such as the Snohomish, Skagit, Snuqualmie, Nisqually and Skokomish. This was the case also with the Chinook of the lower Columbia Valley who supplied fine canoes to tribes far back from the Coast which had no access to big cedar trees. A large canoe for traveling on Puget Sound was sixteen to twenty-four feet in length and there were few of these in pre-settler times. More common were small ones paddled by two women to carry household goods to a fishing camp, gather tule roots or trade with neighbors. They were light and rode low in the water to be easily handled. An even more maneuverable one was built for fishing and hunting ducks and a double-ender was made for river use. There were also one-man canoes and very small ones in which children played and practiced paddling.

When sails were used on long distance travels or when two men went out in a large canoe, they used heavier paddles, the stern one for steering. The second man manipulated the sails which were made of rush matting or cedar bark—a universal material. A wooden or tightly woven bailer was kept handy.

As described by Lewis and Clarke, quoted by George Gibbs in *Tribes of Western Washington and Northwestern Oregon:* "They (Chinook canoes) are upwards of fifty feet long and will carry eight to ten thousand pounds or from twenty to thirty persons. Like all the canoes we have mentioned, they are cut out of a single trunk of a tree which is generally (white) cedar although fir is sometimes used. The sides are secured by cross bars or round sticks, two or three inches in thickness, which are inserted through holes made just below the gunwales and made fast with cords. The upper edge of the gunwale itself is about ⅝ of an inch thick and four or five in breadth; and folds outwards so as to form a kind of rim which prevents the water from beating into the boat. The bow and stern are about the same height and each provided with a comb reaching to the bottom of the boat. At each end are pedestals, formed of the same solid piece, on which are placed strange, grotesque figures of men and animals rising sometimes to a height of five feet, and composed of small pieces of wood firmly united, with great ingenuity, by inlaying and mortising, without a spike of any kind. The paddle is usually from four and one-half to five feet in length; the handle being thick for one-third of its length, when it widens and is hollowed and thinned on each side of the center which forms a sort of rib. When they embark, one Indian sits in the stern and steers with a paddle; the others kneel in pairs in the bottom of the canoe, and sitting on their heels, paddle over the gunwale next to them. In this way they ride with perfect safety the highest waves and venture without the least concern in seas where other boats or seamen could not live an instant. They sit quietly and paddle, with no other movement, except when any large wave throws the boat on her side, and to the eye of the spectator she seems lost; the man to windward steadies her by throwing his body to the upper side and sinking his paddle deep into the waves, appears to catch the water and force it under the boat, which the same stroke pushes on with great velocity."

With the Yurok Indians at the mouth of the Klamath River, canoe building was a practical monopoly. They were the vendors when Tolowa, Karok and Hupa chiefs needed canoes. One reason for this—the tens of thousands of redwood trees covering the sands of the river mouth, the supply continually replenished by winter storms and spring floods. These dead redwoods, the Yuroks believed, made better canoes than the standing trees did as the wood already had some air and sea water seasoning. By spreading pitch on the areas to be reduced and by successive burning, chipping, and scraping, a serviceable if not handsome craft was created. Two men could make a twenty-foot canoe, to carry some ten thousand pounds of weight, in four or five months.

The Yurok canoe, used mainly on the rivers, was round-bottomed, straight-sided with high freeboard, both ends blunt and upturned for better handling in the swift currents. These canoes would navigate rapids safely and go twenty to thirty miles north and south of the Klamath with some degree of stability.

The Baron Karl Von Loeffelholtz's account of his life with the Yuroks at the village of Tsurai in 1850-56 is included in the book *The Four Ages of Tsurai*. He wrote:

PROVINCIAL ARCHIVES. VICTORIA

Partially Woven Cedar Bark Mat and Cape

"Their construction of canoes is more difficult (than the making of tools) but very skillful. For this a piece of a trunk of a fallen, but healthy and completely dry, red-wood tree is taken because it is light weight, easily worked and lasts well in water. Only half of the trunk is used, the heart making the floor, the outside the freeboards. A trunk five feet in diameter is made into a canoe three and one-half feet wide. Fire is used instead of hewing and carving. The burning of the cavities and curves is care-fully controlled and the charred areas are chipped out with sharp stones. This work goes on for months and would do honor to any good carpenter with the best of tools, assuring that a canoe of this sort will last a lifetime. The Indians thus are very care-ful of the upkeep of the canoes and protect them from the sun by filling them with green branches and leaves. A canoe is turned over when it is not in use and covered with branches. If it begins to leak in spite of this, the Indians try to keep it in shape by tying it together at the ends with spruce or willow branches. The sides of the canoe vary in thickness according to the size of the craft. They are from one to three inches thick, the bottom and ends being thicker. The paddles are lancet- or spatula-shaped and about five feet long. A man paddles a canoe either standing or sitting, using both

PROVINCIAL ARCHIVES, VICTORIA

Bella Coola Village

hands and bending the upper part of the body. These canoes are not safe in rough seas and the smaller, narrower ones capsize easily. They do not spring leaks readily because of collisions or the effect of water or air. The outer form of the boats is smooth and elegant, nicely rounded in profile. The bow and stern are decorated by carvings. The boat is usually five to six times as long as it is wide and two-thirds as high as wide.

"The tribe had about five or six canoes for hunting and fishing in the sea. The chief owned the biggest canoe. It was about eight or nine meters long, one and a half meters wide and about seventy centimeters deep. It was turned up at the bow and stern and had rounded, slightly elevated sides and a rounded body. The cross section of the canoe was almost a semicircle at the center. The bottom was somewhat flattened. The sides of the canoe were five to eight centimeters thick and had strips of wood at the upper edge. These strips were bent inward to make handling the boat easier when it was launched or pulled back onto the land. The canoes were made exclusively of redwood, which is soft but resists rotting and cracking well, and is easy to work on. This was imperative since they had neither stone axes nor chisels. All they had for the construction of canoes was a chisel made from stag horn, and fire. They used redwood paddles about two meters long with blades shaped like willow leaves. They paddled with both hands—standing, sitting or kneeling."

PROVINCIAL ARCHIVES, VICTORIA

Bella Coola Bird-Man

Columns and Crest Poles

I T is said of several pagan civilizations—"They had no poets and they died." A corollary may be made of the Northwest Coast Indians. They had neither written language nor any Orpheus to carry their songs and folk tales into immortality. They had inventive ability and imagination but the only forms of expression they had to give their culture a place in history was their painting and carving.

All of the tribes had an innate desire to give some kind of form to the characters of their myths and legends. With the people south of the Fraser River these expressions went little beyond crude paintings on rocks, decorations on the prows of the bigger canoes and, in a few localities, simple figures shaped out of wood for grave markings and spirit signs. It was left to the Northern tribes to develop wood and stone carving to an artistic and spectacular degree.

This art rose to its highest point with the Tsimshian, Tlingit, Bella Coola, Haida and Kwakiutl tribes and dwindled down to poor imitations with the others. The Tsimshians carried it to dramatic perfection in their grave posts, house fronts and detached poles, creating their own designs and adapting those of their neighbors. But old people in their villages, looking at the garishly colored carvings on poles sixty feet high, could remember their childhood when there were no such things.

In that day a crew of Haida sea hunters, cruising into the mouths of the Nass and Skeena Rivers to trade with the Tsimshians, would probably have seen the row of low winter houses unbroken by totem poles. Canoes would be drawn up on the beaches, nets and baskets laid out on the driftwood to dry, but the only evidence of folk symbols would have been in the paintings on the cedar plank house fronts, on the short posts built against them and the small ones standing by the graves.

The carvers in those days were not artists nor was there any profession or pride attached to the work. Making the posts and painting the figures on flat surfaces was merely carrying on a social custom of illustrating the old tales handed down from father to son, and by so doing, making the symbols part of the family tradition.

Myths about the raven, wolf, bear, eagle and thunderbird as clan ancestors were continually being recited and it was only natural for a chief or medicine man to want to show what the birds and animals in the story were like. It is doubtful if any of the tribesmen found any truth in the tales. But why worry about that? Old men entertained children with them and if they could not explain why the eagles they saw fly-

The Tsimshian tribe occupied both banks of the Skeena and Nass Rivers, having as neighbors the Kwakiutl on the south and Tlingit on the north.

ing did not come down and talk as they did in the legends, they gave the best answer they could and no one had a better one. And if one chief was pressed to explain how his great-great-grandfather happened to be a Raven, and another person's a Thunderbird, he might have shrugged his oily shoulders and said: "Well, that's the way it was."

The figures of the frog, beaver, shark, mountain goat, owl and halibut had no further purpose than as displays of rich men or symbols of family pride. They had no spiritual significance, were in no sense idols or fetishes to which the people bowed in reverence. They looked upon the figures as hereditary crests and when a chief ordered a new house post carved to perpetuate his own fame or to commemorate some newly gained power or prowess, they saw a big potlatch coming up with lots to eat, plenty of gifts and fortunes to win at gambling. The story behind the pole meant little or nothing. What went on in front of it after it was raised meant everything. Conversely, it was traditional that any totem pole, no matter how big and impressive it was, if erected without a beach party, would merit no attention whatever and it might as well be broken up for the fires.

There is little knowledge of the early totem carvings since wood rots quickly. Yet there has been evidence that the primitive faces and figures were merely gouged out of the softer woods, chipped or scraped away with pieces of shell and stone tools. The figures took the form of fish and animals as faithfully as the natives could depict them, of huge faces on flat cedar planks, mouth openings being doors to the houses.

The highly stylized art form of totem poles perhaps began with the coming of the Russians and reached its peak about 1875. It was evidenced by the poles being detached from the houses, the tallest one of these being the Sarau-wan or Chief Mountain pole at Gitkas on the Nass River. The native skill fell into disuse soon after, carried on by a few artisians as a means of making a living in a demanding white world.

In the Tsimshian villages on the mainland beaches and more than two hundred miles up the Nass and Skeena Rivers, the houses were usually built in rows facing the water. The detached poles were mounted in another row a few feet in front, each representing the crests and clan symbols of the house owners—the birds, animals and people connected with family history. Sometimes there were two or three poles to a family, erected a generation apart as succeeding chiefs took over.

The poles stood until the bases rotted off and if they began to lean, were left that way, perhaps supported by props. Rarely, if ever, were they replanted or removed to new locations. When they fell, they were left to decay or were burned. When villages were abandoned for lack of food or to avoid depradations by an enemy, the poles were left with the houses.

The Tsimshians liked to make likenesses of the sun in their house front paintings and common types of totem poles carried symbols of killer whales, porpoises, sea lions, ravens and dogs. Other general subjects were eagles, dogfish, white owls and thunder. Many of the poles told the full story of myths and were known by such fairy-tale titles as the Blue Bill Duck Woman, Ten Faces Across the Top and Grandfather of the Red Hair. And many of the private family poles had no formal name other than that of the owner, such as The Pole of Lukawl or The Pole Commemorating Kapskoltsch.

The influence of Hawaiian culture has been noted in the North Pacific totem work, the result of some interchange of migrations of Haida, Tsimshian and Kwakiutl peoples with South Sea islanders. Many families on the Nass, Skeena, even Alert Bay

PROVINCIAL ARCHIVES, VICTORIA

Tsimshian Dance—Skeena River

and Burrard Inlet to the South, claimed to have Hawaiian ancestors. Oyai, known as one of the best totem carvers on the Nass, was said to be of Kanaka extraction.

The name Edenshaw is synonymous with Haida tribal history. There were three generations of chiefs bearing this name, all reputedly good carvers, the middle one being the most skilled with totems and canoe building. Haida poles showed a high degree of individual expression characteristic of the carver.

The poles of the Bella Coola tribe were not as numerous or as tall as those of the Tsimshians and others to the North. Legends were handed down to the effect that their first poles were erected by a group of the first Bella Coola people according to a design given them by the supreme being, Alkuntam, or in a desire to leave to future generations a record of their early experiences. Any chief descending from this group had the traditional privilege of making a pole which included these experiences but this plan was not always followed.

When one of their chiefs prepared for a potlatch and ordered the construction of a pole, he often took liberties with the myths by including symbols of his own exploits or those of a father or grandfather. He might also incorporate in the pole design the name he was about to assume or of a deed he had recently accomplished.

At the top of the pole the Bella Coola carver always placed the bird or animal cloak in which his first male ancestor came to earth. Beneath this was the cloak of

83

PROVINCIAL ARCHIVES, VICTORIA

Mummified Tsimshian Man—Fort Simpson

the mother's first ancestor. In the continuing design he often included the cloak of his wife's original forebear and perhaps the first earthly creatures any of these might have met.

The poles of this colorful tribe were carved from great cedars, the designs standing out in high relief. The carvers were allowed much latitude in choosing designs and paint colors and this gave natural variation to the poles. At the death of an owner, the pole was often removed to the grave to act as a memorial post. If not, it was left until some later owner of the house wished to replace it with a pole of his own.

At potlatches to honor the dead, other variations in carvings were made to depict the achievements of the deceased instead of the living chief's ancestry. One was a grave post much like the house pole, portraying the cloaks of ancestral descension to earth and the family myths, by way of impressing the beholders, especially those from foreign parts. Another variation was a series of plain posts set by the grave to number the major ceremonies given by the dead chief. Still another was a post, painted instead of carved, depicting the goods given away during the man's life—pictures of canoes, coppers, slaves, etc. The daughter of a chief might have been so

PROVINCIAL ARCHIVES, VICTORIA

Nass River Salmon Cache

honored, with pictures of the goods used to rebuy her from her husband. If carved posts were desired, small models of canoes and figures of slaves were mounted on the wooden shafts.

The Coast Salish seemed to abide by no tribal rules regarding the carving and erection of totem poles. They were influenced by the Kwakiutl and other Northern culture, each chief utilizing his own ideas as to what should be included in the sculpture. One pole might be topped by an ancestral allusion and below it would appear a fish or human figure with a hunting bow to represent the owner's skill in these pursuits. Many of the Salish poles and posts were carved by Kwakiutl specialists imported for the purpose but in the latter days the tribe developed good carving skills of its own.

The original Nootkas had no house poles of their own, their early carvings being confined to crude attempts within the houses. They made paintings on boards used as screens or on interior walls of the chief's space in the communal houses, with animals and fish as the dominant subjects. The large carved poles and posts seen by the early explorers were thought to have been obtained from Kwakiutl by gift or marriage dowry.

Eulachon Supplied Nourishing Oil

So oily was this small fish, it could be lighted and used as a torch. During a feast for honored guests, baskets of them might be tossed on the blaze to provide heat and light and as a gesture of prosperity. Eulachon oil was relished by all northern Indian groups, used as a sauce for salmon, halibut, clams, fish spawn and even berries. The eulachon or "candle fish" was a type of smelt, about ten inches long, the main source being the great Nass River runs in the spring.

The Tsimshian caught eulachon by simply raking the big schools with a fish-rake, made of bone teeth fixed into a bar of wood. This was swept through the water from a canoe, the fish being impaled on the points and shaken off in the craft. This was usually done by man and wife—the latter paddling and the man using the rake—or four or five family members would take a canoe and as two raked the others kept it steady in the swirls and eddies of the river and strong downstream winds. Each family used five to ten tons of fish during a winter, some of which might be set aside for trading purposes, and to assure themselves of the supply, they worked day and night during the fish run.

The Tsimshian people had a virtual monopoly on eulachon fishing and, therefore, a great deal of wealth. They were also in a strategic trading position, midway between the versatile Tlingits north, the Haidas with their canoes and sea otters and the Kwak-iutl with their slaves and dentalia shell. In this way, they acted as middleman to the whole northern coastal area and could engage in most profitable trade.

Drying Eulachon

Extracting Eulachon Oil—Nass River

PROVINCIAL ARCHIVES, VICTORIA

"Jek Man Comes"

VOICES droning out songs came from a small house on the fringe of the timber. Inside, men and women were clustered around a fire beside which a half-grown boy crouched on a mat. Another figure was bent over him—a man, naked to the waist with a horn-like band of twigs around his head. When he straightened and moved, his short legs jerked out from the folds of a gaudy-hued blanket.

"The tekejek has the spirit," the man crooned over and over in a muffled voice. "It is still in the water. He fell out of the canoe and his head went against a rock and he makes strange talk. He does not talk like himself at play or work. The tekejek will not let go."

"My son is sick," the father said broodingly. "That is the way he is. What happened since the first snow fell he cannot remember. Now the jek man will shake him free from the water spirit. I have paid him to do this. The jek man comes and he will do this."

That was the way it had happened. And now the doctor—the ichta—turned to the father who could only speak of him as the jek man or the man who had control of the spirits. His loose-skinned face peered through the long curtain of grayish hair and from the dried lips came a shrill squeak. Now he snatched up a rattle in the shape of an unnatural sea creature and shook it violently as he held a wooden mask over his face. It was crudely carved and painted in red and black but none of the watchers knew what it was. Only the ichta knew. He knew what spirit held the boy's head.

Dropping suddenly to his knees, he threw his head and shoulders back as though a tree had fallen on him. This he repeated several times as he shook the rattle and the sweat formed on his belly. The people could see it. He groaned and sang mournfully and talked to the water spirit. The people could plainly see he struggled hard to hold the spirit, to keep him from going back down below. The boy crouched with his hands on the mat and stared at something no man or woman could see.

But the ichta could see. His groans became weird cries and he reached a claw behind him for a strange-looking wooden hook. The crook of this carved stick went around the boy's neck and the bony arms pulled the head to the earthen floor. Then the spirit man threw the hook away and took the small hands, pressing them against his own sweaty skin at the hips and chest. In a creaky voice he called out the names of many fish and water animals.

Two Bears and Chilkoot Blanket

The Tlingit was the most northern tribe of Northwest Coastal Indians, occupying the mainland and island area from Yakutat Bay south to Dixon Entrance and Nass River.

PROVINCIAL ARCHIVES, VICTORIA

Men were beating sticks on box drums, the women as silent and motionless as house posts. Then the boy was jerked to his feet where he swayed uncertainly. His lips were moving at last and creeping out between them were the names of the fish and animals spoken by the ichta. This man was leading him around the fire and the legs of both were trembling. Back and forth, in all directions, the two circled the fire as the words were said and the drums spoke in flat sounds. When the man and boy stopped, the mask came off and the rattle dropped to the earth. In a weak voice the ichta spoke to the father and sank to the mat where the boy stood looking at him in wonder. The tekejek has let him go, the spirit man said. Yes, he is willing to give him up. Now it is done.

*　*　*　*　*

In some such ritual at this, the Tlingit spirit doctors or shamans, effected their cures, dispersed witches and exerted their power over fish runs and storms. They were a strong influence in the people's lives and themselves lived in a world remote. For any man who could consort with spirits must dwell apart from ordinary humans.

The profession of ichta was hereditary, passing from father to son or grandson, complete with masks, drums, rattles and "spirit catchers." Yet the man who was heir to all this must be one with whom the spirits wanted to commune. Ambition to be a great doctor amounted to nothing if the person could not influence the tekejek or kijek or takejek—the spirits of water or the upper regions or the land.

For exercising his power, the ichta was well paid and always in advance. If his incantations and gyrations did not bring about the desired effects, he offered excuses that a strange spirit had interfered and the performance would have to be repeated—upon payment of additional shell money or sealskins.

The ordeal to test a man's ability to become a spirit doctor was rigorous. He went alone into the forest, away from all other humans. For weeks or months, he lived only on devil's club roots and a little water. Should he be so gifted as to meet the spirits sooner than this, he returned, but it was even better if he remained in seclusion until he met the spirit of the land otter whose tongue gave him all the secrets of the profession.

At such an encounter, the neophyte was properly shaken and after making sure this land otter was really of the spirit he killed the creature. As it fell back and died, the tongue protruded. The aspirant cut it off at once and beseeched the spirit to allow him all the ichta privileges including the right to conjure and dance in the accepted manner. He put the tongue in a basket and hid it securely so no designing person would find it and rob him of his spirit powers.

If after a testing period in the woods, no spirit appeared to the seeker of magic, he went to the grave of the departed ichta whose place in the tribe he sought. He slept there one night, then took a tooth from the skull or part of a small finger and held them in his mouth. Then, gaunt to the point of exhaustion after his long vigil in the forest, he returned to his people and announced his retreat had brought him success and he was ready to prove his spirit control. If he did prove it, he could accumulate great wealth. If not, he could look for the spirits to turn on him and destroy the human form of a charlatan.

It was traditional with the Tlingit ichta to look the part of a spectre. He let his hair grow long and made no attempt to groom it. He wore bizarre-colored sashes and blankets, awe-inspiring face masks, carved bone spikes on his head and was equipped with a rattle or charm for every sickness, food shortage or storm trouble. The conjuring of a spirit usually took place around a fire and involved wild dances with violent contortions. He had special names and songs for every jek and professed his ability to throw any spirit into the body of anyone doubting his powers. This would cause the scoffer to faint or go into a fit.

A legend is told along the Nass of one ichta who, to prove his intercourse with the spirits, insisted upon being thrown into the sea. Accordingly, he was wrapped in matting which was securely tied with a strip of otter skin, his supernatural power symbol. He spoke to the spirit four times and the body was lowered into the sea with a long line attached to a float. When the line went slack the watchers in the canoe waited for their ichta to signal he was ready to be pulled up. No signal came even after the sun had set and they paddled shoreward to mourn his loss.

The next day the people went back to the spot where the bladder had been floating and could see no sign of it. Three more times they returned and on the fourth saw the spirit man hanging by his feet from a cliff, his face covered with blood as the sea birds flapped around him and tore his flesh. The men cut him down and on the journey to the village the ichta regained consciousness. The people were then convinced he did indeed have great affinity for the spirits.

During the new or full moon periods in the winter, ceremonials were conducted by the Tlingit spirit doctors to make full peace with the powers of land, sea and upper regions on behalf of the whole village—to ward off illness and bring good fortune to everybody including the ichta and his relatives. These rituals were followed by feasts lasting many days.

For several days before the demonstrations, all the relatives helping him cleaned themselves inwardly with sea water and put feathers down their throats to induce vomiting. On the appointed day they neither ate nor drank but cleaned the great man's house and put new planks by the fire. Then they started singing and beating on drums. The ichta appeared in elaborate ceremonial attire, ran around the fire, doubled his body until it seemed almost to break, always keeping time to the rhythm of the drum beat, always with his eyes on smoke curling up through the roof hole until the vitals themselves seemed to be coming out of his head. Then he would suddenly jerk to a stop and scream. The songs and drum sounds ceased, for the spirit in the man was ready to talk.

Sometimes this ceremony was varied to include a mock chase, a pursuit of the spirit man. While drums were being pounded, hundreds of people singing on the two or three levels in the house—fully clothed men and women on the upper tiers, naked men with daggers on the lower—a curtain was drawn aside to reveal the ichta with hair and cape flying as he sped around the fire.

The singers then changed their tones to ones of despair, and with knives raised high, made gestures of pursuit, the ichta squirming and dodging in pretense of terror and abject flight. He would snatch a burning log from the fire and hurl it toward the roof of the house. The dagger men would turn upon the other singers and then upon the spirit man, at length catching him in a net and tying him down. The symbolic ceremony ended when he was covered with a mat and dragged back behind the curtain amid a chorus of groans and moans.

Crest Poles and Symbols—Ketchikan

Hawkan Burial Ground

Graves at Ketchikan

Exposing witches was within the province of the Tlingit spirit man and he went about this with all the heathen gusto he could command. The men or women harboring the evil spirits were found out when they tried to obtain some parts of their victims in order to cast a spell of sickness, death or other harm upon them. A man might wish another to go blind and so coveted a lock of hair, some spittle or dirt scraped off this unsuspecting person. He would take this token to a graveyard and secret it in a body before cremation or in the ashes after the burning. And with the act he would perform maledictions to transfer the dead eyes to the man he wished to harm.

In time the victim might feel his eyesight failing and if he suspected he was bewitched, he would send a messenger for the jek man. This dignitary, recognizing the symptoms of witchcraft, would order the house of the afflicted person to be thoroughly cleaned. Then he gathered his helpers, clad himself in his religious robes and with all his rattles and drums visited the house. Against a background of singing and booming, he manipulated the abdomen of the victim to force out the evil spirit or sucked at his flesh to draw it out. When the singing and stick beating stopped, he was supposed to know who had cast the witchcraft and forthwith accused this person of the evil.

Unless the accused man had powerful friends or relatives, he had little chance of pleading his cause. His hands were tied, palms out behind his back, and he was dragged to some isolated hut or cavern and left without food or water. In two days he was given the chance to confess and if he did not, was forced to drink sea water and left to the ravages of slow death. If he did confess, with or without guilt, he was taken to the place where he had secreted the hair or body dirt of the bewitched man. Left alone, but under close scrutiny, he was expected to retrieve the objects from the corpse or ashes. When he did, he placed the pieces on a segment of bark or leaf and showed them to the watchers. When they were convinced that these indeed were the offending objects, they allowed the witch man to run to the beach. Knee-deep in the water, he turned to the sun four times as he held up the bewitched property. Then dropping them, he walked out farther and submerged himself four times, calling out that the sick person would now be well. Then he himself was free to return to normal life.

When the accused was an influential man or had rich relatives, they would beseech him to release the evil spirits and not force them to torture him. He had a chance. In the rigid caste system of the Tlingits, and in varying degrees throughout the whole social scheme of the Northwest Coast Indians, wealth was synonymous with survival.

NOWELL PHOTOS, BANCROFT LIBRARY

PROVINCIAL ARCHIVES, VICTORIA

Graves at Sitka

Grave Figures—Sitka

Graves at Wrangel

Prow of Tlingit Canoe

Sealskin Drying in Tlingit Village

NOWELL PHOTO, UNIVERSITY OF WASHINGTON

OREGON HISTORICAL SOCIETY

PROVINCIAL ARCHIVES, VICTORIA

UNIVERSITY OF WASHINGTON

Tlingit Houses

Skak-ish-stin—Tlingit Woman

CASE AND DRAPER PHOTO, BANCROFT LIBRARY

Kaw-Claa—Dressed for Tlingit Dance

CASE AND DRAPER PHOTO, BANCROFT LIBRARY

Tlingit Spirit Doctor and Sick Woman

Soul Catchers of Tlingit Spirit Doctors

CASE AND DRAPER PHOTO, BANCROFT LIBRARY

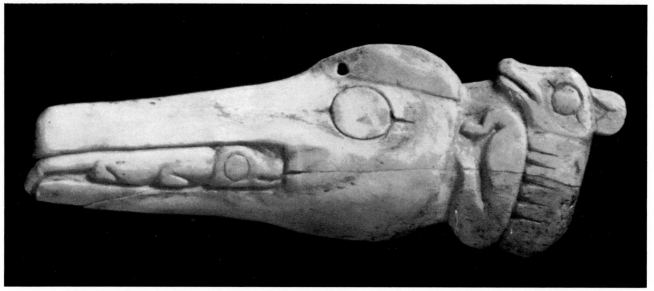

PORTLAND ART MUSEUM

Bone Amulet for Curing Sick—Tlingit

Tlingit Dancers

Ichta Spirit Helper—Tlingit

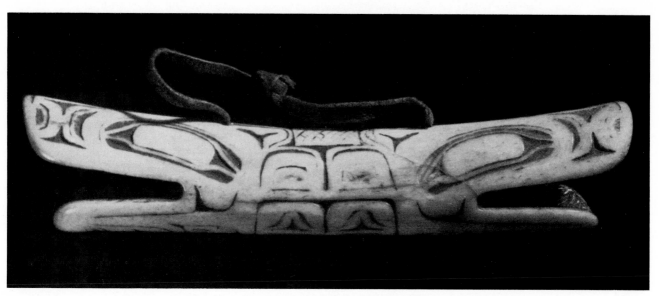

SEAGRAM PHOTO, KETCHIKAN

CASE AND DRAPER PHOTO, BANCROFT LIBRARY

Tlingits in Dancing Raiment

Memorial to Potlatch Giver

CASE AND DRAPER PHOTO, BANCROFT LIBRARY

102

Tlingits Arrayed for Potlatch

CALIFORNIA STATE LIBRARY

CASE AND DRAPER PHOTO, BANCROFT LIBRARY

Tlingit Healer at Dyea, Alask

Dah-clet-jah—Yakutat Tling

In Kodenaha's House—Klukwa

Caw-dik-ney—Tlingit Chief

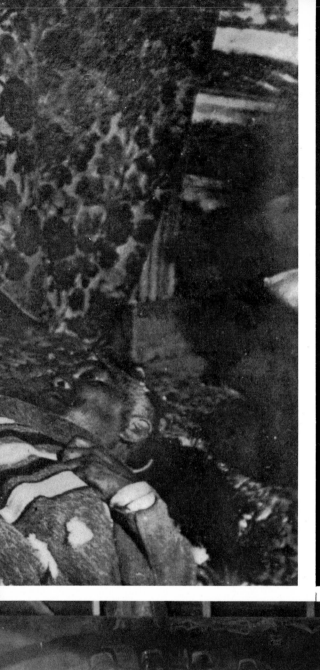

Frog Figure on Ketchikan Grave

PROVINCIAL ARCHIVES, VICTORIA   PORTLAND ART MUSEUM

Tlingit Fish Trap Figure

PORTLAND ART MUSEUM

Dead Man Spirit Mask—Tlingit

PROVINCIAL ARCHIVES, VICTORIA

Nootka Deer Head Mask and Rattle

Nootka

As a sea hunter, the Nootka chief might well look to his noble birth and make the most devout proclamations to the spirits. He inherited his rank from his father who had trained him to be a proficient whale killer and it was his solemn responsibility to lead in the hunt and inspire young men to become great whalers themselves.

If out of laziness, physical weakness, cowardice or inability to work supernatural magic, he failed in these functions of a chief, the village would suffer for want of food and oil and his prestige falter to a point of shame. Then, in spite of his royal heritage, he could be deposed by an ambitious and skilled harpoon man.

The killing of whales was of vital concern to the Nootka and neighboring tribes —Quileute, Quinault, Clallam, Makah and Chemakum. It controlled the people's very existence, made them contented or miserable, the villages prosperous or poor. The men hunted seals and sea otter, fished for salmon, cod and halibut but the whale kill meant not only food but a demonstration of skill and bravery, providing proof that the chief was concerned with the welfare of the village and entitled to retain his kingly respect.

Custom demanded that the chief harpoon the first whale of the season, bring it to the beach where proper ceremonies made it fit to eat and distribute it to the families. After that, lesser men could bring in their own whales. Sometimes, when the chief had a brother with whaling ability, he was accorded the right to kill the second.

The harpooner was not necessarily a person of high rank but he was a person of high standing and some wealth. His skill was derived not only from long years of trial and error but also from earnest communication with supernatural powers. Without certain magical gifts, he might well fail to inspire the tribesmen even though he occasionally brought in whales. And it required wealth to build a whaling canoe, equip it properly, secure loyal paddlers and a good man to handle the floats.

Although members of the whaling crews were subject to many restrictions and taboos and must undergo severe training, it was only the whaler or harpooner who made profound obeisances to the whale spirit. For many days before the hunting season began, he removed himself from his wife's bed and made frequent incantations to the powers of the sea, moon and south wind. As the day of the first hunt approached, he ate sparingly, wore a head band of cedar bark painted red as a token of humility and fell into moody silences.

Nootka territory was the larger central portion of the west coast of Vancouver Island, which included Barclay Sound and Alberni Canal, Clayoquot and Nootka Sounds. Across the Strait of Juan de Fuca was the Makah branch.

Several times a day he went to some secluded pool with a large fan of green spruce on his head and a rattle in his hand. Splashing and rolling in the water, he scrubbed and scratched his body with a handful of hemlock twigs until all the paint and dirt were gone and the skin was raw and blood-streaked. During this display, he sang and made bold promises of great homage to be paid when the whale was killed —and it was always assumed the whale wanted to be killed. Quoting from Volume 5 *British Columbia Heritage Series*, the whaler might make an appeal such as:

"Whale, I have given you what you are wishing to get—my good harpoon. And now you have it. Please hold it with your strong hands and do not let go. Whale, turn toward the beach of Yahksis and you will be proud to see the young men come down on the fine sandy beach of my village at Yahksis to see you; and the young men will say to one another: 'What a great whale he is! What a fat whale he is! What a strong whale he is!' And you, whale, will be proud of all that you will hear them say of your greatness. Whale, do not turn outward, but hug the shore, and tow me to the beach of my village at Yahksis, for when you come ashore there young men will cover your great body with bluebill duck feathers, and with the down of the great eagle, the chief of all birds; for this is what you are wishing, and this is what you are trying to find from one end of the world to the other, every day you are traveling and spouting." As he scraped and offered whale songs, his wife sounded her amens —"This is the way the whale will act."

After the final bathing rite, the whaler returned to some normality, including his wife's bed, and in the early morning the whole family aided in the preparation. The whaler's hair was knotted behind his head and on the crown of it was twisted a ring of hemlock twigs. Over this a special hat was placed, one woven by his wife of the small roots or inner bark of the spruce, cone-shaped with a small knob at the peak. When her man had wrapped a black bearskin around him and she had watched him join his seven crewmen and launch the canoe, she retired to her house. Others could work and play but it was proper conduct for her to recline on a new mat and partake of no food or drink until the hunter returned with his great prize.

The crew, made up of competent commoners, all loyal to their chief, had stowed the gear into the thirty-five or forty-foot cedar canoe with great care so that the line and floats would run out without fouling and were paddling the sturdy craft out through the breakers. The harpoon in the bow could be a fourteen-foot shaft of yew wood, some three inches in diameter, heavy enough to pierce the whale's thick hide when given a solid thrust by strong arms. The blade of the head was often a mussel shell bound with whale sinew and cemented with spruce gum to a barbed piece of bone. A short lanyard of whale sinew ran from the head along the shaft, held lightly to it by a few easily-broken threads of cedar bark. The lanyard was bound by nettle fibres to several fathoms of plaited cedar root line. Each succeeding length was smaller, the end attached to the prow of the canoe being about one-half inch diameter. Spare lines were carried in the wide belly of the canoe where were stowed also the twelve or fifteen floats made from the skins of hair seals. These were attached to the harpoon lines as were smaller floats for buoying up the whale's head for towing. These skin bags, inflated by lung power, had been soaked in water for many days previous to the hunt.

The real test of a whaler's skill was not so much in thrusting the harpoon, which primarily required great shoulder and arm strength, but in knowing the exact time to do so. Whales ran in schools, swimming, diving, rising to the surface to blow spumes of air and water high over their forty- to sixty-foot backs, then diving or sounding once more. If the whaler and crew had been faithfully religious before the hunt, the wounded whale could be expected to turn toward shore so the killing could be finished close to the beach.

When a school was sighted, the canoe was paddled swiftly and steered to the outer circle so the attack could be made suddenly from behind the unsuspecting whale. The harpooner marked with his eye the most accessible target and ordered the canoe put on the left side of it. The water of the Nootka whaling grounds was the entrance to the Strait of Juan de Fuca where the winds, waves and tides set up vicious conditions. The harpooner stood with his left foot on the bow thwart, his right forward on the gunwale, the harpoon held crosswise in front of him at almost shoulder height. He waited until the whale had spouted again or showed signs of going down, pivoted and plunged the heavy shaft into the thick hide just behind the left flipper. If the whale sank an instant before the thrust, it was made into the water over the disappearing back.

Instantly, the whaler fell back and down from his perch as the canoe sheered off, clear of the rolling and thrashing whale and floats bouncing out on the sea. This was the most dangerous time. The massive creature, weighing forty or fifty tons, might turn toward the small craft and smash it in one blind rush or a man might be caught in the bight of a line and dragged to his death. If the wound was shallow because of poor aim or sudden canoe movement, crew and canoe were in trouble.

After the violence had subsided, the shocked whale would normally sound, go plummeting down to deep water as the Nootka float tender paid out his lines and air bags. Presently the water would be turning red and the whale would be surfacing in another spasm of anger and pain. Then a second harpoon thrust would be made before the next dive. As big an animal as he was, he struggled against loss of blood and a great pull of air and it would not be long before he came up for the last time and the waves broke over his exhausted body.

Sometimes a second whaling canoe, with a relative of the chief whaler in its prow, would accompany the hunt and be conceded the privilege of planting the second harpoon. A smaller canoe might also be brought along to pull out the first lance and carry it back to the village as joyful evidence that a whale had been struck. The chief whaler and his supporting canoe might have to follow the whale, darting in to sink more harpoons with short lines and floats, until all struggles ceased. A lance with a wide, chisel-like blade was used to sever the tendons of the flukes to render the whale even more helpless and another with a large bony point was driven in behind the flipper to the heart. Then the great creature rolled, spouted blood and died. Holes were gouged into the upper lip and lower jaw to tie the mouth tight so the carcass would not ship water and sink. Then all that remained was the laborious task of towing the quarry home to the village. All too frequently, he had headed directly out to sea and the crew had an extra day of heavy paddling.

A Nootka tale is told of a whaler who as a member of a chief's canoe crew was jealous of the prestige and position of the leader, an inferior harpooner. With dreams of tasting the latter's glory, the would-be usurper organized the other canoe men in a mutinous scheme. The story has elements of man-made romance but has become a lively legend. They waited until the chief had taken a whale and when he leaped out on the creature's broad back to set a harpoon and small floats, the crew swiftly pulled the canoe away and sped for their village with the story that the chief had been drowned, that they had tried to save him and failed.

The whale, they surmised, had been killed far enough from shore for the currents to carry it south rather than into the Strait. The assumption was correct. The whale did not float up on the beach, the chief was presumed dead and ceremonial rites conducted. The usurper proclaimed himself chief.

The old chief, out on the whale, was not dead. If he was not the most intrepid and skillful harpooner, he was resourceful. When he saw his traitorous crew pulling the canoe away and paying no attention to his commands, he knew he was solely at the mercy of a floating whale in a capricious sea. Yet he had talked to the whale's spirit before starting out on the expedition and he talked again now, making fabulous promises if the whale would take him safely home. The whale had cooperated well thus far and would surely continue to be friendly and helpful. He himself had only to stay with the whale.

This he managed to do by cutting a hole in the carcass with his bone knife—a hole big enough to admit his legs and thighs, yet not deep enough to pierce the bladder and destroy the animal's buoyancy, which was enhanced by floats trailing from the harpoon. This shaft was firmly embedded and gave him a steadying grip for his hand. Now he could not fall out, had only to wait until the whale was washed up on some beach. He had no food problem since eating was only a matter of gouging out a piece of the exposed blubber. His thirst he would have to conquer.

The drifting went on for endless days but eventually the Nootka saw a high ridge of land and at length his strange craft struck the breakers. He had been battered roughly by the sea, his throat and mouth caked with salt but he was alive and strong enough to tell his story to the Indians who seized upon the whale. The chief recognized the tribesmen as ones with whom the Nootkas had traded canoes and furs and although they spoke in another language he was able to make their chief understand where he came from and that he must return to his village and set matters right. The Chinook chief, with the prospects of a whale feast and the chance of being presented with a new canoe and perhaps slaves, agreed to take the Nootka home.

When the whale had been divided, the festivities completed and the oil stored in the same sealskin floats which had brought the body to them, a canoe party set out up the coast. The return was an occasion of great triumph. With great acclaim, the old chief was welcomed back and the ambitious usurper sent to eternal damnation, his arms and legs ripped from his torso and burned in many fires.

On days of a Nootka whale hunt, a lookout was sent from the village to a point on some headland where he had a wide view of the sea. When he could detect a familiar canoe towing the trophy homeward, he ran quickly to the village and joy spread like wildfire. All available canoes were immediately launched and assisted in getting the whale to the beach, the men singing songs of triumph and pounding their paddles against the sides of the canoes. The men, women and children on shore climbed to the roofs, singing and shouting as they drummed sticks against the planks.

Once the whale was beached, the ceremony of cutting up the carcass began. The man who had killed it marked out portions for his crew and for those of other canoes who had helped bring in the kill. His own share was a wide section of the back next

PROVINCIAL ARCHIVES, VICTORIA

Nootka Whalers—Clayoquot Sound

to the fin and it was removed first being treated with great ceremony and respect. The whaler could not eat it or surely he would find disfavor with the spirits so he ate a small piece of the tail while his wife sang and danced in front of him.

On the fifth day a blubber feast was given for all except the whaler and his wife. The guests did not take home what they could not eat as by normal custom, so these leftovers were thrown into the sea for the scavenger birds and fish.

The blubber was boiled in wooden boxes by dropping very hot stones into the water, the oil skimmed off and stored in skin bags made from the stomachs and bladders of whales and sea otters. The cooked blubber was smoked, dried in the sun and stored for future use.

Homage to Quahootze

IN a narrative account of some three years as a favored slave of Maquinna, Nootka chief, John Jewett gives his version of a religious ceremony of thanks to the tribe's Supreme Being. Jewett was one of two survivors of the crew of the sailing ship "Boston" captured by the Nootkas in 1803. Reference to the full account is given in the bibliography at the end of this volume.

"On the morning of the 13th of December, commenced what appeared to us a most singular farce. Apparently without any previous notice, Maquinna discharged a pistol close to his son's ear, who immediately fell down as if killed, upon which all the women of the house set up a most lamentable cry, tearing handfuls of hair from their heads, and exclaiming that the prince was dead, at the same time a great number of the inhabitants rushed into the house armed with their daggers, muskets, etc. enquiring the cause of their outcry, those were immediately followed by two others dressed in wolfskins, with masks over their faces representing the heads of that animal; the latter came in on their hands and feet in the manner of a beast, and taking up the prince carried him off upon their backs, retiring in the same manner they entered. We (Jewett and Thompson) saw nothing more of the ceremony, as Maquinna came to us, and giving us a quantity of dried provision, ordered us to quit the house and not return to the village before the expiration of seven days, for that if we appeared within that period, he should kill us." (In later pages of Jewett's journal he continues his description of the ceremony as he saw it a year later.)

"Their religious celebration which last year took place in December, was in this commenced on the 15th of November, and continued for fourteen days. As I was now considered as one of them, instead of being ordered to the woods, Maquinna directed Thompson and myself to remain, and pray with them to Quahootze to be good to them, and thank him for what he had done. It was opened in much the same manner as the former last year. After which all the men and women in the village assemble at Maquinna's house, in their plainest dress, and without any kind of ornaments about them, having their heads bound around with the red fillet, a token of dejection and humility, and their countenances expressive of seriousness and melancholy. The performances during the continuance of this celebration consisted almost wholly in singing a number of songs to mournful airs, the king regulating the time by beating on his hollow plank or drum, accompanied by one of his chiefs seated near him with the great rattle. In the meantime they eat but seldom and then very little, retiring to sleep late, and rising at the first appearance of dawn, and even interrupting this short period of repose, by getting up at midnight and singing. It was terminated by an exhibition of a similar character to the one of last year, but still more cruel. A boy of twelve years old, with six bayonets run into his flesh, one through each arm and thigh, and through each side close to the ribs, was carried around the room, suspended upon them, without manifesting any symptoms of pain. Maquinna, on my enquiring the reason for this display, informed me that it was the ancient custom of his nation to sacrifice a man at the close of this solemnity in honor of their God, but that his father had abolished it and substituted this in its place.

EDWARD L. CURTIS PHOTO COURTESY
CHARLES E. LAURIAT CO.

Ceremonial Bathing—Nootka Whaler

"With regard to their religion, they believe in the existence of a Supreme Being, whom they call Quahootze and who, to use Maquinna's expression, was one great Tyee in the sky, who gave them their fish, and could take them from them, and was the greatest of all kings. Their usual place of worship appeared to be the water, for whenever they bathed, they addressed some words in form of prayer to the God above, intreating that he would preserve them in health, give them good success in fishing, etc. These prayers were repeated with much more energy on preparing for whaling or for war. Some of them would sometimes go several miles to bathe, in order to do it in secret. The reason for this I could never learn, though I am induced to think it was in consequence of some family or private quarrel, and they did not wish what they said to be heard; while at other times they would repair in the same secret manner to pray. This was more particularly the case with the women, who might also have been prompted by a sentiment of decency, to retire for the purpose of bathing, as they are remarkably modest. I once found one of our women more than two miles from the village, on her knees in the woods, with her eyes shut, and her face turned toward heaven, uttering words in a lamentable tone, among which I distinctly heard 'Wocash—Adwelth', meaning good Lord, and which had nearly the same signification with Quahootze. Though I came very near her she appeared not to notice me, but continued her devotions, and I have frequently seen the women go alone into the woods, for the purpose of addressing themselves to a superior being, and it was always very perceptible on their return, when they had thus been employed, from their silence and melancholy looks."

115

EDWARD L. CURTIS PHOTO COURTESY
CHARLES E. LAURIAT CO.

Bathing Before Whale Hunt

PROVINCIAL ARCHIVES, VICTORIA

Nootka Potlatch Welcome Figures

Nootka Boy in Solitary Fishing Ritual

Canoes at Nootka Potlatch

Nootka Woman—Barclay Sound

PROVINCIAL ARCHIVES, VICTORIA

Barclay Sound Nootkas

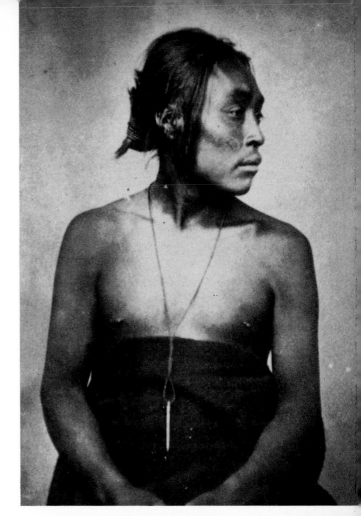

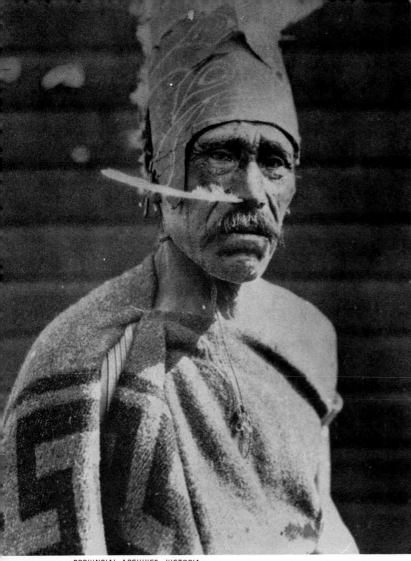

*Nootka with Headdress
and Nose Ornament*

PROVINCIAL ARCHIVES, VICTORIA

It is estimated that about twenty-five groups of the Nootka tribe lived on the western shore of Vancouver Island in an area between Cape Cook and Point Renfrew. There were many villages in the sheltered bays and inlets and although the same basic language was spoken— a language related to that of the Kwakiutl—the people of one section appeared to have difficulty conversing with those of others. This led to frequent disputes and a constant state of hostility.

The Nootka type was inclined to be lean in stature, the faces round and full showing high cheek bones, noses flat with wide nostrils, eyes and hair black, mouths round with lips thick. The men were better at taking fish and sea animals than they were forest hunters and

were especially skilled in whaling. This was probably related directly to the fact that they were skilled builders and handlers of the cedar dugout canoe and this craft, together with the wrapped-twine method of basket weaving, was one of the most highly developed of the Northwest Coast tribes. The Nootka women also made cedar bark, and rush matting and robes in great quantities which served as the utility item of clothing for men and women.

Their houses were of two general types. In the northern sections were the gabled structures, roofs supported by large posts, and in the south smaller shed-like houses, ten to twelve feet high at the back sloping to seven or eight at the front, with walls of planks laid horizontally.

PROVINCIAL ARCHIVES, VICTORIA

Whaler's Ceremonial House

Nootka Woman in Cedar Bark Robe

EDWARD L. CURTIS PHOTO COURTESY
CHARLES E. LAURIAT CO.

Nootka Basket

Nootka with War Spear

Nootka Whalers' Hats

PROVINCIAL ARCHIVES, VICTORIA

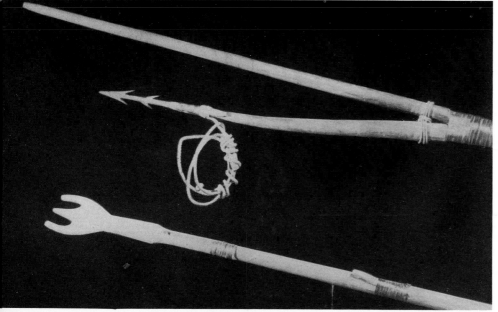

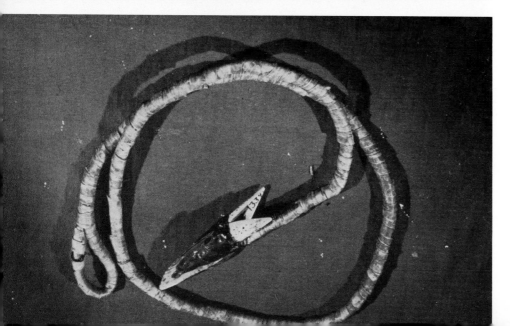

Nootka Face Masks

Nootka Whaling Harpoon,
Sealskin F l o a t and Line

Nootka Fish Spears

Detachable Harpoon Head—Noo

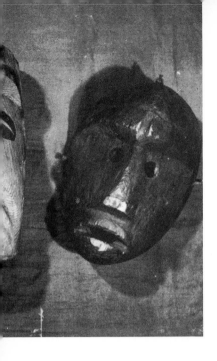

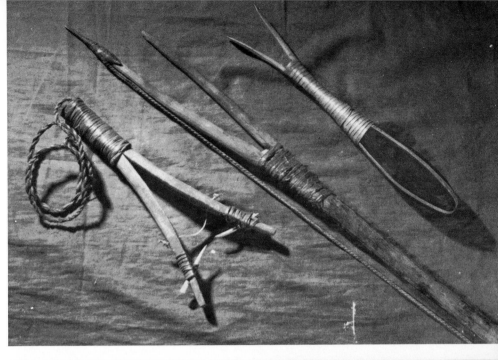

Nootka Fishing Implements

*Sea Otter Bow,
Arrows and Quiver*

Dentalia Spear and Shells

PROVINCIAL ARCHIVES, VICTORIA

PROVINCIAL ARCHIVES, VICTORIA

Partially Butchered Whale—Makah

Makah Whaling Canoes

WASH. STATE HISTORICAL SOCIETY

Whaling was Life Itself

LIVING on the Cape Flattery tip of the present Olympic Peninsula, across the Strait of Juan de Fuca from the Nootkas, the Makahs were not considered Coast Salish. They spoke the Nootka language and had similar racial characteristics. Yet they were adjacent to Salish people, traded with them and drew from them many habits of living. They were whalers by trade whereas most of the Salish tribes hunted the big animals by whim or circumstance.

The entire life of the Makah people evolved around the whale. The meat represented much of their food, the oil relish for other foods and a trade item of the highest importance. In addition, the killing of whales furnished one more way to social prestige and wealth and made the harpooner a man of envy and strength.

He did not achieve this high place through luck or ambition alone. He rose to the noble height by training from childhood and strict adherence to a code of behavior and certain rituals which gave him supernatural powers. He was usually a chief, inheriting his position from his father, obligated by rules, regulations and intense training to carry on this high calling. If he could not meet the rigorous demands of the whale spirit, if he did not show the necessary will or courage to be a great whaler, there was usually a relative or rich man in the village properly endowed with the whale power, to take his place—by potlatch and public declaration.

The whale hunt was the greatest event in the seabound communities and the beaching of the great animals presented an occasion for profound rejoicing. The carcass was properly strewn with white down and the whaler marked off the portions due his crew and the men of other canoes helping in the kill. The part marked for himself and family was the wide section of the back next to the fin and this was removed with great care and reverence. This meat the whaler could not eat as he would forthwith lose all whale-hunting skill. For eating purposes, he had a small piece of the tail. During all this butchering process, the whaler's wife and women relatives sang and danced on the beach, the process being followed by a blubber feast.

Clothes Came from Trees

THE house was so big the Makahs had pulled a forty-foot canoe inside to repair breakage and there was plenty of room around it for the seven families. The men were out fishing now and all of twenty women were making cedar mats and dog's hair blankets.

Each family lived in a section on the raised platform running around the walls. Each was separated from the others by knee-high partitions, some of boards, some of matting, and in one or two the families' possessions were arranged in orderly fashion or out of sight in chests. Most were in sad confusion, a jumbled array of paddles, nets, skin bags of oil, whaling apparatus, boxes, baskets of dried fish and blubber.

The women working with the bark wore shell in their ears and their dark faces were streaked with darker paint and tattoo lines. Some wore cedar bark skirts, others merely waist bands and their bare skin glistened in the dim firelight.

All spring the village women had been gathering cedar bark. They chose the smaller trees, under a foot in diameter, ones with smooth trunks and few branches. With a mussel shell blade, one would girdle the tree at knee height and slip a sharp stick into the cut, running it up as high as she could reach. She did the same on the opposite side and pried the bark out until she could get her fingers under it. Pulling gently, she would loosen the piece and work it out until all of it was free of the tree, repeating the process on the next side. The tree would die and the men would use it for firewood. There were plenty more for all the bark anybody would want.

At the end of a day, each woman would have enough bark for several carries to her house. And after peeling off the rough outer bark to expose the smooth inner layers, she would let this dry in the sun or before a house fire for several days. Between trips to strip more trees, she would roll up the thoroughly dried bark for cutting into strips and making baskets or save it until she could start making matting.

That was what the twenty women were doing now. They had made the tools themselves—six-inch sticks, half inch in diameter, for shredding the bark; larger ones for beating it. These were two feet long, six inches wide, half inch thick with one edge rounded. Each woman used two of the small sticks between the fingers of one hand to pull the bark into shreds.

Squatting on the earthen floor, a woman laid one of the two-foot boards in front of her on a block of wood. With the bark resting on the board, she raised the other one and struck it downward so that its edge slid down the side of the stationary board, bruising the bark. After each blow, her left hand fed the material over the rounded edge.

For hours she kept up this constant shearing and pounding until the whole mass of bark was pulverized and softened. Although individual threads were broken, the tensile strength of the whole sheet held it together.

Now, a Makah woman would ask herself—do I want this bark for clothing or matting? If for the latter, the only further work to do was to spin it into a thick cord on a spindle. The cords formed the warp strings of blankets or mats. For clothing, the bark was beaten still more with pieces of stone or bone with grooved faces.

The spindle consisted of a rod three or four feet long inserted in the center of a whorl or circular wood disc, eight or nine inches in diameter. This disc fitted tight to the spindle two-thirds of the way down its shaft. The whorl acted both as a fly wheel to aid rotation of the spindle and collar against which the finished material was wound. The joined ends of the ball of bark thread were attached to the spindle at the whorl, which was then rotated to wind the two threads into rough yarn. Tension was maintained on the threads by passing them over a smooth stick or through a ring before they were attached to spindle.

The weaving was done on a simple loom made of two horizontal rollers revolving in wooden frames. The warp was kept apart by a thin strip of wood, allowing passage of a hand. It was run around rollers in a series of continuous cords so the web could be pulled around as often as desired, the weaver working from top down.

Cedar bark for matting was woven from flat strips in a "checkerboard" pattern. Strips were of even length, folded over at the middle, with one half at right angles to the other. Light cords of nettle fiber or grass bound them together at the folds. Mats had greatly varied utility, were used for bedding, making summer shelters, protecting canoes and cargo from the hot sun and for house partitions. Makah designs were worked into them by dyeing some strips in a mixture of charcoal, oil and water.

For ceremonial uses, red colors were needed and such dye was prepared from alder bark. Pieces of it were soaked in water and urine, heated by hot stones. Fresh alder was added until the mixture was deep red. When cooled, the pounded cedar bark was soaked in it and dried.

By their dress the people made known their position in the village. A man wearing only a simple breech-clout was at once identified as a commoner going about his wood-cutting or fishing. A woman wearing a bone ornament in her nose, perhaps with vertical tattoo lines on her cheeks, her legs covered with an apron of cedar bark shreds, was quite obviously of a rich, w ell-blooded family. One wearing a sealskin robe could be no less than the wife or daughter of a chief.

On the ordinary day when the weather was mild, people in the villages avoided clothes. Their bodies were well greased to discourage flies, their skin and feet well conditioned to the earth and elements. The men preferred to wear no clothes whatever except when the weather was bad and upon such state occasions as potlatches.

Rain called for broad-brimmed hats woven of cedar roots and these were worn by both men and women when paddling canoes, the men fishing and women traveling to kelp beds and clam beaches. Trousers and moccasins were not native dress but the traders having contacts with inland and mountain people took on some of the dress customs on occasion.

But it was the potlatch and winter dance ceremony that brought out the frills and finery. The tribe had a fine sense of pride and people wished to appear prosperous in the eyes of guests. Many sea otter robes and deer skins were laid away for such use only and women spent long winter hours sewing bird skins together. Men were equally vain and often arranged trades with foreign tribes to obtain clothes never before seen by their own people. Normally, clothes made the man uncomfortable but the Indian still believed clothes made the man.

PROVINCIAL ARCHIVES, VICTORIA

Makahs Beaching Dead Whale

Quileute Types

WASH. STATE HISTORICAL SOCIETY

Salish Women on Trading Trip

UNIVERSITY OF WASHINGTON

PROVINCIAL ARCHIVES, VICTORIA

Potlatch—about 1915

Cleaning Salmon—Neah Bay

WASH. STATE HISTORICAL SOCIETY

Coast Salish Tribes of Puget Sound

THE people of this general area west of the Cascade Mountains, extending south and west of Puget Sound, were considered to be a part of the Nisqually nation, with language similarities. Of limited population, the Samish, Lummi and Nooksack lived around Bellingham Bay and Lummi Island—the first two salt water type tribes, the Nooksack being river Indians.

The Skagit tribe, with several subdivisions including the Swinomish, covered the area on both sides of the Skagit River and San Juan group of islands, were distinctly canoe people, whereas the Skykomish toward the Cascades were mountain hunters. To the south were the Snohomish with which were numbered the Snuqualmie and other minor village areas. On the western shore of the Sound were the Chemakum, and Clallam.

Flanking the southern end of Puget Sound were the major tribes of Nisqually and Skokomish, each adjacent to those rivers. On the Duwamish River, the mainland opposite and a few islands, were the Duwamish and Suquamish. To the south around the headwaters of the Chehalis River were the Willapah and west of them to Grays Harbor on the Pacific Coast, the Chehalis tribe. South along the Lewis River to the Columbia, lived the Klickitat and Cowlitz. In this whole Puget Sound area, from the Fraser River to the Columbia, there were some thirty major and minor tribes.

A grey, December day with one of them can be imagined with an early morning sound of fire sticks being rubbed together in the dry bark dust. There was no light in the big lodge except from this flickering blaze, which eventually became a vigorous fire, and from others springing up in the house. Shadows crossed each other on the mat-covered cedar plank walls as dim figures with bare feet walked soundlessly on the earth floor. Women might be climbing ladders or reaching up to the ledges where winter food was stored. Within a few minutes, the men would be rising sleepily from the floor mats, staring into the fires, warming their hands in the heat and smoke which now filled the big area and escaped through two holes in the roof which sloped to the rear.

These were common people and they dressed simply. The men mostly had slept in nothing at all, covered with cedar bark or woven dog's hair blankets. Some now drew on skin leggings which were tied around the waist and ankles. Over their shoulders they pulled fur capes if they had them. The women wore cedar bark skirts but only the old ones had covering above their waists. Children snatched up what they could find, infants crawling nakedly over the dirt.

There was conversation by one fire. The man who owned the house where the eight families lived had suddenly gone away on a trip to get himself a new wife and some of the men were thinking of cutting down his house post outside. They were angry that he had not taken some friends with him and they would like to cut the post down. Some of the men said they would move to another house. The women laughed. They knew it was only talk. Nobody would move. It was winter and they had little else to do but talk.

"How much food do you have?" one woman asked. She was young and her hair was parted in the middle, hanging loose over both shoulders, the ends braided and tied with buckskin. Her face was greased, painted with red and brown streaks. The second woman said there was plenty of food, if anybody needed some. The face of this one was tattooed with parallel lines on the cheeks. No, the first woman said again, there was no need of food. She had plenty of dried salmon and seal fat, some roots and huckleberry cakes. But this day, she said, was a good one for several women to go to the storehouse in the woods and bring more food to the house.

As they talked, the women were carrying things to the cooking pit outside, spreading dried meat and fish and tule roots on the ashes of other fires, covering this with fir boughs and dirt. From inside one of the men brought fire on a flat stone and laid it with dry sticks on the covering. By this time the stones of the fires inside were hot and were dropped in baskets of water. It boiled at once and heaps of dried salal berries were scooped in. The boiling stopped and more hot stones were added to start it again.

The people ate under the benign countenances of the several animal and bird faces carved and painted on the house post. They scooped the hot berries and liquid into mouths already full of meat and fish picked out of the hot ashes. A watertight basket of tea made from dried huckleberry leaves was passed from hand to hand and everybody ate until their stomachs were full. It was a good time. Everybody had plenty of food. Everybody was satisfied. Even the scowling men would be glad to see the owner of the house come back with a new wife.

Food governed almost every action in the lives of the Salish people, as it did those of the other Northwest Coast tribes. Like animals, they were content with full stomachs, remaining close to a plentiful supply or moving to where they could get more and better food. There were a lot of fish in the rivers and at the mouths of them—several kinds of salmon. The best were caught in the spring and the flesh was dried and smoked. The women cut the fish open, saving the eggs to eat with seal oil. Heads and tails were cut off, the skin left on the rest. After splitting, the backbone was taken out and the entrails thrown to the dogs. The strips of fish were fastened to sticks and smoked over smudge fires of green hemlock and spruce, usually in sheds near the winter houses. The backbones were dried over fires and sucked by the children. The heads were a bonus, eaten raw or boiled.

Smelt and herring were netted in the breakers and dried in great quantities. Some tribesmen caught sturgeon, others cod and rock cod. When the beaches were kept clean by the changing tides, mussels and barnacles were large and juicy. Clams, oysters and crabs were eaten fresh, made tastier with seal grease. The seals were not the fur bearers of the north but were those covered with sleek, brown hair. When caught, the animal was rolled around in the fire until his hair was burned off, the skin scraped and the fat removed. This was eaten fresh when necessary or worked down to oil, the meat usually boiled before eating.

There was a brisk traffic in food between the Puget Sound tribes. The Nisqually Indians who had an overabundance of clams would journey fifty miles to trade them to one of the interior tribes such as the Klickitat for elk and deer meat. The Skagit and Snuqualmie who hunted extensively came down from the mountains to trade with the villagers on salt water.

Deer and elk were highly prized over other animal meats such as beaver, mountain goat, bear, wildcat, cougar—all of which were shot with bow and arrow or snared —and over birds such as ducks, grouse and pheasants, which were netted or speared. None of the tribesmen killed eagles, gulls or hawks as these had special spiritual significance. Deer and elk were the only meat dried and this was done with special care by hanging the pieces on frames around which fires were built.

The women gathered the vegetable foods. With long, tough sticks they probed the earth of marsh and meadow in the fall for fern roots. Cattail or tule roots were eaten raw and the camas bulbs of the flat prairies, tiger lily and wild potato bulbs steamed in pits, dried and stored in baskets cached high in the trees. Many berries were gathered — salmonberries, huckleberries, blackberries, salal, raspberries, wild strawberries. They were eaten fresh and dried on cedar bark mats spread over fires. Often they were mashed in large baskets, dried and molded into flat cakes which would keep indefinitely. Hazel nuts were stored in the ground or if shelled, kept in tree baskets. Acorns were shelled, boiled and buried in salt water mud. When taken out to eat, they were soaked in fresh water. Acorns, fern roots and sprouts of salmonberry bushes—but never hazel nuts—were eaten with salmon eggs. Camas bulbs were often boiled with salmon and other fish.

There was food in abundance and when the people took the initiative to go fishing and hunting and gathering nuts and berries, they ate well and lived happy lives. But there were always raids by slave-hunting tribes from the North, feuds with neighboring villagers and the ravages of sickness inadequately treated. There was to come a day when the fish swam unmolested and black bear came down to the beaches to sniff the decaying timbers of Indian houses.

Siletz Indians in Dance Attire

OREGON HISTORICAL SOCIETY

OREGON HISTORICAL SOCIETY

Chief Stokin—Cascade Tribe

Slaves were Trade Goods

THE chief announced that eight men and six women were going north to meet some Chehalis. They were going to take some women slaves, some dentalium shell they had obtained from a party of traveling Nootkas and they were going to bring back a hunting canoe and maybe some deer meat. He said they were going to leave when the sun started to set and the tide was ebbing. They would make several sleeps on the way to Shoalwater Bay.

The Indians were Chinook living on the north shore of the Columbia River bar. They were setting out to trade with their more or less friendly neighbors up the Coast because trading was their business. They always saw to it they had a liberal supply of the two most wanted items—slaves and dentalium shell—and since it was easier to get things by trading than by fighting, they were forever on the move to dicker. Living at the mouth of a great river flowing into the sea, with many tribes bordering it for hundreds of miles and others reached by sea routes, they had prime trading territory.

What made this activity successful was that all the tribes liked to exchange goods and to show the visitors how friendly and rich and willing to gamble they were. It was a gala day when the home guard Clackamas or foreign-talking Yaquina people saw a fleet of Chinook canoes approaching. Welcoming shouts would go up, the fires lighted and everybody would make a scramble for his best clothes and a hasty inventory of food. And it is doubtful if any visiting or receiving tribe thought it would get the worst in the ensuing trade and games.

The most reliable Chinook trading commodities were the slaves. They were ever in demand and most of the Northwest Coast tribes were not warlike enough and too permanently settled in villages to make a practice of pillaging and robbing to get slaves. Several of the Northern tribes did make slave raids by stealth and a show of force but the main source of this chattel came from the California and upper Columbia River tribes who obtained them from predatory plains Indians. This supply was augmented by local feuds and slavery status into which the poor and luckless would often sink.

The rule of "once a slave, always a slave" was held inviolate in the rigid social structure of the West Coast tribes. He or she was property in every sense of the word, although considered valuable and worthy of protection. Owning slaves signified relative wealth or war prowess and made daily living easier. No owner, except in a fit of fury or madness, would willingly beat a slave or even work him to death. If he did, it was in a show of riches and power—a man so great he could afford to kill some of his slaves.

On the other hand, this male or female creature had no rights and was subject to all demands and whims of his owner and family. The children of slaves were slaves in turn and even the children of a slave and a tribesman in good standing were only half free. Even if a slave was lucky and was given the means to purchase his freedom, he was never fully accepted as an equal. And it was usually tribal custom to kill some or all the slaves of an owner upon his death.

The slave system was a vicious circle, at once a help and a hindrance. Wars, feuds, raids and trades were made to get slaves and wars, feuds, raids and more trades were made by rival tribes to get them back. The slaves often ran away or were stolen by some third tribe or by the chief in the next village of the same tribe. Every slave owner was in a constant state of anxiety—which he did not display—to keep his charges busy and safe.

Many slaves came into that miserable state by committing some crime and being unable to pay compensation or by going insolvent by gambling or foolish living. All crime, including murder, could be expiated by payment in shell money or goods and no person except a chief was exempt from this possibility. It was not uncommon for a man to have as slaves his own father and mother and for them to be treated with all severity.

A Quileute or Tillamook Indian chief, on a trading expedition to the Columbia River, could instantly tell whether the man and woman he took as slaves were of Chinook blood—by the shape of their heads. At birth most Chinook heads were flattened, a custom extending to the Cathlamet, Clatsop and even to Puget Sound and Northern tribes, and a slave with a round head would naturally be of a foreign tribe.

Immediately after birth, the infant was placed in a trough-like cradle lined with moss, the end where the head rested being slightly raised. A pad of cedar bark was placed on its head and over this a strip of skin which was laced tight to the wood of the cradle. As the head expanded over a period of a year, the press caused the head to be elongated. During this process the child's eyes bulged out to resemble large glass beads but he was supposed to suffer little pain. Once the pressure was removed and the head shown to be properly flattened, it did not revert to its original shape.

Chinook wars to obtain slaves were hardly worthy of the name. Having become prosperous and respected by other tribes for their trading skill, they chose to settle most differences by arbitration. The war threat was half bluff and half a means of satisfying the restlessness of the young men. Having once determined to strike an enemy who had attacked camp and carried home some slaves the Chinooks had originally stolen, a chief would send ferocious young men out to warn the hostile tribe. They would make fierce gestures and perhaps shoot a few arrows at dogs or old women and otherwise give notice that their chief would seek revenge on a certain day. This was an ultimatum to fight or be ready to pay damages for the stolen slaves.

On the appointed day, the Chinook chief's war party would arrive by canoe fleet, braves dressed in heavy elk hide armor or bodies wrapped in wooden strips bound together with bear grass and wearing cedar bark helmets. Women and slaves would be huddled in the sterns of the canoes, ready to carry the payment goods—as these were expected without bloodshed. While the young men brandished weapons and shouted menacingly, the chiefs went into a parley, sometimes through a third party who acted as mediator.

If night fell before any agreement was reached, the Chinooks camped on the hostile beach as the firelight flickered on the angry faces of each side. For most of the night voices shrieked and abusive threats were flung back and forth. Perhaps morning brought no settlement and flaring tempers could be contained no longer. The women and children would be dispatched to safety and the fight would start. It was generally not a violent battle to the death. When one or two men were knocked out of their canoes or took spear wounds in their legs, the leader of their forces would probably throw down his weapons and declare the contest at an end. If the Chinook warriors had lost, they would paddle home without redress but vowing they would return for a more successful foray. If they had won, they named the terms and the enemy would be forced to pay.

The greatest fortune a slave could have was a family with wealth and influence. If a son or daughter of such a family was carried off and put into bondage, the parents suffered more disgrace than sorrow. If he or she had not been taken beyond traveling distance, they would equip a canoe with gifts and money, pay homage to the captor and redeem their offspring. Then after appealing to the spirits to cleanse them of dishonor, they would take the son or daughter back into the family home.

A Chinook legend concerns a trading expedition up the Columbia to the Klickitat country. Among other items purchased was a twenty-year-old woman. She resisted attempts by her new owners to get her into the canoe and on the voyage down river, twice tried to drown herself. The Chinook was forced to tie her to trees at night camps.

Listening to her defiant cries, the chief's daughter recognized some of the words as the same used by an old man slave her father had. She talked to him, learning that he too had been a Klickitat and made him teach her to speak a few words in that language. She then made friends with the woman captive and by the time the party reached the home camp she had made up her mind to set her free.

During the night she prepared a canoe for the escape, placed in it a basket of dried fish and berries, cut the slave's cords and then told her to bind her own hands and feet around the tree. In the morning the chief found his own daughter tied fast and heard the story in her own confession. The chief did not untie her but called for a bark rope and began lashing the girl's naked body. The ordeal was interrupted by people rushing to the river bank. A canoe had been sighted, being paddled toward the village by the old Klickitat slave.

When the canoe grounded on the shore, the slave told the villagers he had escaped with the girl but she had surmised what would happen to the chief's daughter when he learned what she had done. She said the Klickitat would have to take her back to the chief and if he refused she would drown herself. This she could now do easily.

When she was taken to the chief's daughter she said she needed only one true friend in life and she would rather be a slave to this royal daughter than to live in poverty at home.

She was not taken into the Chinook tribe with pomp and ceremony. Her head was round. However, before the cold season set in, an avenging party of Klickitats came and in the early morning surprised the Chinook chief's house, wounding him and carrying away both his daughter and the Klickitat girl.

The legend ends there but it cannot be imagined the incident did. The Chinook now had his honor at stake. So the slave raids went on and on.

Rush Mat Summer Houses—Chinook

Columbia River and Coast Tribes

AS active traders in slaves and dentalium shell, the Chinook Indians spread their fame far and wide. They lived on both sides of the Lower Columbia River and had frequent contact, friendly and otherwise, with the smaller and less aggressive tribes on the north shore of the river—the Kwalhiokwa, Cowlitz and Klickitat—and with divisions of their own tribe on the south shore—Cathlamet, Clackamas—and farther up river—the Cascades, Hood River, White Salmon, Wishram and Wasco. They carried on spirited relations with the Shoalwater tribe on Willapa Harbor and the Clatsop south of the Columbia mouth.

On the Pacific Coast south of the Makahs on Cape Flattery, lived the sea-hunting tribes of Quileute, Quinault, Hoh, Queets, Copalis, Humptulip and Lower Chehalis. South of the Columbia were the Tillamook, Siletz, Yaquina, Alsea, Suislaw, Lower Umpqua, Coos, Upper Coquille, Tututni and Chetco. Inland, extending to the Cascade Range, were the Tualatin along the Willamette River, Northern Molala, Yamhill, Santiam, Lakmiut, Mary's River, Yonkalla, Upper Umpqua, Southern Molala, Takelma, Klamath, Shasta and Modoc.

Grave of Chief Concomly—Chinook

Chinook Camp—Mt. Hood across Columbia

OREGON HISTORICAL SOCIETY

OREGON HISTORICAL SOCIETY

Clackamas Twins

142

The Chief
Gives a Potlatch

IF he was a Tsimshian, he may have "called the people in" to prove to them he had not made false promises to some visiting Bella Coola dignitaries. If he was a Haida town chief at a time when food was scarce, he could have told all the commoners he was giving a potlatch and a feast. Perhaps the head man of a Cowichan settlement had died and his brother, upon becoming chief, wanted it known with hard emphasis that he was now leader and everybody would look to him in all important matters of their lives.

The potlatch was all things to all the Northwest Coast tribes, a ceremonial with a hundred purposes. The institution was basically the same with all of them, varying according to tribal tradition, the temperment and ambition of the giver. The word "potlatch" is from Chinook jargon meaning "to give" and that is essentially what the event of the potlatch was—the giving of many presents. It was the motive behind the giving that colored every proceeding.

Ruling families of Indians used the potlatch for publicity medium, court, welfare agency, loan office, aid to economic and social advancement. Its principal function was to establish tribal prestige, class distinction, family honor and privilege. The chiefs accomplished these ends by public declaration and distribution of gifts to everyone in the local village and all other villages who were invited to the ceremony. The more a chief thought he had to defend or the greater his desire to impress, the more people he sent for and the more gifts he made. A lavish outpouring of blankets and skins was the only method he had to show his people his right to assume new duties and privileges or to continue with current ones, to commemorate the building of a new house, the birth or naming of an offspring or the granting of new names to them as they attained puberty or adulthood.

The importance of the potlatch increased with the latitudes and the fact that it was a more potent force in the North and gave certain backbone to tribal progress may have been one of the reasons why those Northern people were tougher and resisted longer. The tribes on Puget Sound and south used it mainly for humanitarian and friendly purposes, distributing gifts to the needy and by such generosity gaining stature with the people. A Chinook chief might give a potlatch to satisfy a claim of family honor. A Skagit chief might have great need to establish the fact that he was the wealthiest man of a tribe and so displayed his riches by giving away everything he possessed. He did not necessarily expect repayment for even though he paupered himself he was still the wealthiest man.

Such unselfish attitude thinned out with the Northern tribes. With them it was more vital to increase social standing or to establish firmly whatever standing the chiefs had. A major potlatch, for example, could raise a man from the status of com-moner to that of petty chief, provided he had enough fluid property or could borrow it for the occasion. Or if the caste system of a tribe was too rigid for this, the pot-latch could be used to show wealth and power within the common ranks.

With the Tsimshians, who were very class conscious, the potlatch assumed great importance. They used it for all manner of reasons, from a simple gathering for the first naming of children, confined to the mother's relatives, to elaborate intertribal fetes when a chief took over as the head of a large village and was required to im-press all the other rulers. And such a potlatch was a colorful and exciting event.

Imagine the amount of work involved to entertain two thousand guests, many of whom had traveled for miles by canoe. When a chief told his family and all those living in his house: "Quahklah is too old to hunt sea otter or fish or tell anybody else what to do or when dances are to be held. He knows he no longer has the power of a chief and says he is willing to see a new one. I am his cousin and Laxs-gik (of the Eagle clan) and strong and know what the people need. I will give a pot-latch and everybody will know I am the new chief and then I will give a feast and many gifts and maybe I will show how much more power I have than Quahklah and he will be able to see I have the right to be chief."

For months after such a pronouncement, all members of the ambitious cousin's family and his wife's family worked diligently to be ready for the big days. Feeding all the people meant having ready great quantities of fish and meat, berries and roots, mussels, clams, eulachon oil, herring spawn and soopalally. The men fished, hunted and made cedar food boxes. The women dried the fish, made berry cake and wove baskets to store the food in. Singers and dancers were arranged for, masks and fam-ily crests freshly painted.

A week before the potlatch the tribal canoes began arriving, men arrayed like great birds and animals with gaily colored wings a-flap, and each day saw the beach more crowded. Hundreds of canoes might be drawn up on the sands and as many fires flickering among the cedars and firs. As the day of the potlatch approached, the men worked off their restlessness with singing and gambling.

The ceremony began with a long speech by the aspiring chief. Several of his own canoes may have been pulled up close to his house and planks laid across them on which he stood. Or a special platform may have been built and decorated with the family crests, or totems, and the chief's coppers. Piles of blankets and other goods would be stacked around the platform and members of his family ready to distribute them at his command. All the guests would be sitting or standing in circled groups within the sound of the host's voice.

The chief would shout that he now had the right to be the new chief and he had called the people together so he could prove it. He was rich and powerful and while the present chief had been good in his day and brought them winds and fish and sealskins, that day was gone now. It was necessary to have a new chief and he was the man. He wanted the right to use a new name and to receive the proper crests of a reigning chief. And to show he was going to be a big-hearted chief, he was going to make many gifts.

The parcelling out of the gifts could have lasted all day. First the old chief would be overwhelmed with blankets, canoes, dentalium shells, abalone shells, bows and

arrows, halibut hooks and salmon spears. He would have no possible use for this wind-
fall but if he were to be forever silenced, never offer any threat to the chieftainship, it
was necessary that he accept all these gifts. And the throngs might be witness to
a heart-breaking spectacle—the old chief fading visibly as the young one flooded him
with a thousand blankets and a ton of implements.

It is possible to imagine that somewhere in this press of humanity was another
ambitious chief of minor stature and he too would have made known his claim to
the office of chief. If so, custom demanded that he too accept an array of gifts until
he was speechless, his claim retired until such time as he could amass enough wealth
of gifts to embarrass his erstwhile benefactor.

If this chief refused to be overwhelmed and persisted in his right to the chief-
hood, the present potlatch giver might think it neccessary to further humiliate this
rival, to actually degrade him in the eyes of all the people and thereby rise firmly
above him. He would then continue to pour out gifts to the man and members of his
family until the very value of them staggered him—an amount he could never hope
to repay. The rival would be obligated to accept all this or be forever disgraced. If
he refused the great bounty, he could well disappear or kill himself as others had
done. If he took the gifts and accepted defeat, the new chief would then seal the occasion by the dramatic gesture of smashing the finest canoe he owned, breaking up
or throwing into the sea his most precious "copper"—a family crest carved or painted
on a copper or wooden shield. Such an act would never be forgotten by his people.

Once the giver of the potlatch had satisfied himself that he would have no in-
terference from any disgruntled tribesman and that he was now officially the new chief,
he ordered the fires lighted, the feasts and singing and games to begin. Men draped
in fringed blankets woven into the intricate designs of the "Chilkat" type depicting
animals and supernatural beings, would begin a slow, high-stepping movement around
a fire or totem, ending the dance in frantic, breathless action. A loud chorus of singing would carry across the beach where cedar bark mats were spread on the sand and
the leaders in gambling games shook their bones and rattles.

The breaking or discarding of coppers had special significance to the Tlingit,
Haida, Tsimshian and particularly to the Kwakiutl. The copper itself had slight intrin-
sic value, being merely a shield hammered out of metal or a slab of wood on which the
family crest was carved or ornamented with marks of a Tsimshian secret society such
as the Dog-eaters or Fire-Throwers. Yet a copper had tremendous value to its owner
as a symbol of riches and power. To show his wealth a man may have paid a thousand
hair sealskins for a copper and each time it was given away and purchased back its
value increased. And when in some dramatic display of venom or proof of superior-
ity, a chief destroyed his copper, everyone within sight understood the deep significance of the act.

The aggressive Kwakiutl tribe used the potlatch for hard and fast purposes.
The system allowed the chiefs to maintain a continual "cold war" with their blood relatives. When a ruling family wished to put out goods for investment, a potlatch was
held and the usual gifts made. Although presented with all friendliness, the gifts bore
interest and were expected to be repaid with this interest. The rate for a few months
was about 20% but perhaps, in the case of a newly born child, the rate for a year
might have been 100%. In some vital situation where a chief was savagely deter-

OREGON HISTORICAL SOCIETY

Siletz Indians in Full Dress

mined to eliminate all contenders for his position as leader, he expected gifts returned in value two or three times that of which he gave.

The man who made the gifts had no way of enforcing payment but he rarely had occasion to demand it since default meant complete loss of "face," shame and disgrace for the receiver and family. No self-respecting Indian could afford this for it could well mean being cast out of the tribe or into a slave condition and sold out of the tribe. In fact, Kwakiutl history records instances of suicide, murder and warfare due directly to the vicious practices of the potlatch. On the credit side, it sharpened competition and lent stability to this powerful tribe whereas decay ate into softer, easier-going people to the south.

The Kwakiutl also used the institution as a court. In ruling circles, a man who could speak more fluently than his chief or being a disinterested party could make statements his superior could not, made a flamboyant platform performance. He pled the chief's case before the people, persuading them that such and such was true and that they would be forever damned if they believed otherwise. There was no judge to decide the case. The people themselves did that by silence or murmured assent.

Haida life revolved around the potlatch and feasts were invariably a part of them. In times of want or in cases where some families found themselves hungry, a chief could gain great popularity by seizing upon this opportunity to gather food from those who had plenty and invite everyone to a potlatch with the express purpose of eating heartily. In gratitude, the families being benefitted would improvise songs and dances which the chief could absorb into his family traditions.

Most common to Haida custom was the potlatch given by a chief to members of his own clan when a new house was built or when he was tattooed with designs of profound meaning or when his children had their lips, noses or ears pierced and pieces of bone inserted. A special si'ka potlatch was given when a chief had died and his successor built a tomb or set up a grave post.

Many chiefs, unable to supply riches of their own for a potlatch, borrowed from their wives' treasury. Since this involved opposed clans, one borrowing from another, the potlatches often became long-enduring chains of cross exchanges, resulting finally in victory and riches for the sharper side, poverty and decline of social standing for the less wary.

Nootka potlatches became extravagant and colorful displays in the efforts of chiefs and their children to rise higher in the social scale and in authority. One of the chief features of the whale hunt with these people was the parcelling of the carcass by potlatch. The whaling chief took the section directly behind the head for himself (although custom decreed that he himself could not eat it) and sectioned out other parts for those he favored or wanted under obligation to him.

Whale hunting was a dominant force with this tribe and a whaling chief had always to be respected and obeyed. Should his skill and power at sea hunting begin to slip away, he might call the people to a potlatch and declare publicly that such tales told about him were not true. Or he may have owned a valuable slave and mistreated him until the tormented creature had leaped out of a canoe and drowned himself. To show the people that the slave had been of no use and that he still had wealth enough to buy as many slaves as he wished, he invited all his countrymen to a party and feast.

Blankets and skins were standard potlatch gifts but there were others. One narrative concerns a man receiving ten songs from the chief of another village. The songs were purported to be composed by the chief but sung by some of his henchmen. The retiring chief took title to the songs and added them to his family records, then gave a potlatch to double their value, giving the composer twenty blankets. These blankets therefore had a potlatch value of thirty or forty songs.

Who was to be present at a potlatch? That was for the person giving it to decide. With the Nootkas, a chief might call a council of his immediate family and make an inventory of all articles to be given away. Then villages and the important people in them were discussed and decisions made. The chief and his party would set out in canoes to visit the various settlements, calling the names of invited guests as the craft was beached. The common people were included in large potlatches since mass approval was often needed.

Mourning for the dead was observed in Tlingit potlatches, as upon the death of a chief, and could well be a series extending over a period of a year or more. When a Raven chief died, the opposing society of the Wolf conducted the burial rites because the father of the dead man had most likely been a Wolf. The Ravens then would give a potlatch to reward them and to officially proclaim the new chief. The potlatch was continued after a month or so on the completion of a house for the new chief. Another would be held at the erection of a memorial post at the old chief's grave. If the Wolf men had been asked to help carve the post or put a guarding fence around the grave or build a shelter over it, the potlatch gifts were meant as both payment and thank-yous.

Only the slaves could ignore the potlatch.

And the Canoe Was a Tomb

The canoe served the Chinook and lower Columbia River tribes in death as in life. It was at once a symbol of a man's living days and a conveyance to take him across the dark river under the earth to whatever spiritland he was going. And it was a handy place to put the body so animals and casual enemies could not disturb it.

In the mass burial places, on high ground or promontories of the river, a man's canoe was lifted as high as possible into the forked limbs of trees or mounted on posts. After the body had been placed in it, some of his earthly possessions were piled alongside or hung on stakes below. The extent to which burial ceremonies went depended upon the social status of the dead person. Common people were accorded few rites; slaves none.

The death of a chief, however, called for proper pomp and ceremony. If he had used several canoes in life, he might be buried in a small one, a larger one inverted over it and his big war canoe covering both. Near the grave his tomahno-us or spirit board would be placed conspicuously and around it arranged most of his prized possessions—after they had been rendered unusable. The mourners who gave up all this family wealth and paid the burial costs may have been all but pauperized.

There was a division of a man's property, however. During his life, whatever a man used, whatever were considered his belongings, were his alone. Even the blankets he used were his private property and his wife had no share or interest in them. She had her own mats and baskets and could keep all her earnings except any from prostitution. These belonged to her husband.

So a wife did not expect to gain anything from a man's death. The male relatives took charge of the burial rites and what possessions were not destroyed or deposited at the grave site were distributed among mature sons and others. And when women died, their graves were undistinguished or marked very simply by a cup or camas stalk or piece of clothing. The bodies of children were often merely hung in baskets.

For some seasons after the death of important persons, Chinook chiefs gave some attention to renewing the grave ornaments from time to time. Common people were satisfied to have their relatives' bones removed after the flesh had sloughed away or dried up, to have them wrapped in new matting. Tribesmen took care there was no violation or pilfering of valuables at the grave of relatives.

With some subdivisions of the Chinook up the Columbia, burial customs did not include the canoe. Bodies were wrapped and placed in caves or rock niches with the head to the west where the road to mi-mel-us-illahee —the country of the dead—lay. The Cascade Indians built vaults of pine or cedar planks with slightly sloping roofs and these also lay east and west. They wrapped their dead chiefs in skins tied with grass or bark and placed them on mats. Erecting poles on the vault roofs, they hung on them belongings of the dead, decorating the inside walls and doors with carved or painted figures to represent the ones buried there.

OREGON HISTORICAL SOCIETY

Chinook Lodge—Lower Columbia

OREGON HISTORICAL SOCIETY

Chinook Canoe Tomb

OREGON HISTORICAL SOCIETY

Columbia River Rock Carvings

Klamath River Tribes

THE five main groups of people which comprised the southernmost tribes of Northwest Coast Indians were those on both sides of the Klamath River—Yurok, Karok, Hupa, Wiyot and Tolowa. The Wiyots on the Mad River and Humboldt Bay, the Tolowas as far north as the Smith River.

The Yurok tribe occupied the land from the juncture of the Trinity and Klamath Rivers to the coast. They were a highly developed people, heads slightly flattened, skins almost black and in stature were inclined to be pudgy, the women handsome in childhood and youth but quickly losing their beauty. Their hair was worn smoothly combed, unplaited, fastened at the brow with strings of shell and falling over the shoulders.

Yurok houses had round cellars, four or five feet deep, about twelve in diameter, covered with a square cabin of split poles with flat slabs for roofs. The door was cut out of a four-foot slab with stone and elkhorn tools—a round hole just big enough to allow one person at a time to crawl through. The space in front of the house was swept clean, sometimes paved with cobbles, where the women sat weaving baskets—small ones of willow twigs and pine roots for holding acorn flour or large ones for carrying burdens on their backs.

Acorns were a staple food from which bread and mush was made. These were nuts from the chestnut oak. After shelling, the meat was scorched, then pounded on stone in a bottomless basket. Water was poured over the flour and the mixture placed in small sand pools on the river beach around which fires were built. The process leeched the bitterness out of the flour and when the cakes were partially hardened the sand was brushed off.

The Yuroks netted wild ducks in lagoons, smelt in shallow pools. When the sea was quiet, the canoes would work out a mile or two for shell fish and algae. The men were timid hunters, believing devils to be lurking behind the trees, but they were bold and fearless in canoes. In making these they had a monopoly, selling and trading them to the Karoks and other nearby tribes.

There were tens of thousands of big redwood logs on the beaches of the lower Klamath and they made better canoes than the standing trees. The men spread pitch on the part they wanted to reduce, burned the wood deeply, extinguishing the fire with wet bark. The canoes were not big or handsome but they were serviceable and with them they could shoot the Klamath rapids and go twenty or thirty miles up and down the coast with great cargoes of trade goods.

The word "Karok" meant "up the river" or "up East" and this signified where their villages were—up the Klamath River from the Yuroks. The people were well-

upa Tribal Leader

COURTESY MRS. PERCY L. BRYAN
A. W. ERICSON PHOTOS

knit physically, legs stronger than arms, bodies with almost feminine roundness. The men wore simple buckskin girdles, the women loose garments of braided grass from breast to knees. The latter tattooed their chins with three narrow fern-leaf lines. They wore the hair in two clubbed queues, pulled them forward over the shoulders.

The Karok men were brave and cunning, curious and quick to imitate practices they liked in other tribes. They were not cruel to wives and children but indifferent. They were likewise quick to take offense, very vindictive and above all avaricious, believing money would "cure every ill." Their basis of wealth was dentalium shell, the tips ground off, so pieces could be worn on strings which were sometimes as long as three feet. Red woodpecker scalps also had a definite and high value.

Karok men built the lodges, killed game, constructed fish weirs in the rivers, caught salmon and spread it out to dry, cut and carried firewood, helped gather acorns, nuts and berries, made bows, arrows and fishing gear. They congregated in sweat-houses which were underground assembly chambers or council houses with flat roofs a few feet above ground. They entered these airtight, stuffy areas through small hatchways and slept or grouped themselves around the fire which burned endlessly, telling tales and passing village gossip. No women were allowed, except in an emergency a female shaman might be permitted to examine a sick man. In the summer they lived with the women in common wickiups.

Women were almost a common possession before marriage but after becoming wives they were carefully watched. Adultery was practiced, however, usually compensated by money payment. The women gathered wood for cooking, dug roots, carried burdens, wove baskets and made clothing. They were drudges yet the men would help them and look after the children when not at work or on journeys.

Unlike the northern tribes, the Karok villages had no chief with great authority. A rich man had certain influence and was considered the leader but he did not have complete control except on a war mission. Then one man was placed in charge and his orders were obeyed. On these forays, often to avenge some considered wrong, the fighting was ragged and unorganized. Some of the warriors used bows and arrows, others jagged rocks which they were adept at throwing. Scalps were taken but not heads. And the fighting might stop suddenly if one side decided to capitulate by the payment of money.

The Hupa tribe lived on the lower reaches of the Trinity River and were of a high type after the manner of the Karoks. They were very valorous and held many tribes in a near vassal state. They dressed, lived and fished like the Karoks and Yuroks, considered dance ceremonies more important than war. They had no chief in a dominant sense, even for war, but did have well-developed laws for fishing, hunting and nutting. Their lands were rich in acorns and manzanita berries.

They were a highly immoral people yet with them adultery was a serious offense. For it, a man's eyeballs might be pricked so they would eventually waste away. The guilty woman was not punished but any bastard child resulting was shunned by everyone. He was not used as a slave but had no family privileges and could marry only another bastard. Yet even he could gain certain social status if he could win at gambling. The Hupas kept no record of time, measuring ages by guess—so many "moons, snows, sleeps."

The people living on the Mad River and Humboldt Bay were the Wiyot—a pudgy, black-skinned race with small eyes, low foreheads and distinctly guttural speech. In

A. W. ERICSON PHOTO, COURTESY MRS. PERCY L. BRYAN

Sweathouse at Pec-wan—Yurok

general they indulged in much inbreeding with resulting tribal weakness of intellect. They were prey to ghoulish and frightful superstitions, believing that ghosts dug up the dead, carried them to the forest where they extracted poisons to destroy the living. These evil spirits had the power to turn people into dogs, coyotes and ground squirrels. The Wiyot lived on very rich agricultural lands, raised many healing shrubs and gathered mosses, lichens, flowers and vines.

The Tolowas dwelt north to the Smith River area. They too were deeply superstitious and to them every object, living and inanimate, had spiritual power. They considered heaven to be somewhere in a high place back of the sun and hell as a dark, dismal place in the bowels of the earth beset by all manner of pests, fiends and calamitous weather.

These people were bold, haughty and aggressive, spreading terror among the Yurok villages to the south which they raided frequently, killing the men and capturing women and children. To an even greater degree than with their neighboring tribes, money absolved all misdemeanors and avenged all wrongs. Their acquisitiveness went so far that even low characters, unfit for any good use, could win high stakes in a gambling game and take over a chief's position. In common with the Yuroks, Hupas and Karoks, the Tolowas placed high value on the appeasement of the spirits by their winter ceremonials and ritual dances.

The Ritual Dances

THE dances of the Indian tribes in the Northwest area of California—the Yurok, Karoks, Hupa and Tolowa—were a very real and moving part of their lives. Most of them expressed hope, appeals for peace, prosperity and abundance; were soul-baring efforts to placate the evil spirits which ruled the air and showed their anger in the storms and other natural acts of violence.

The dances were not an outlet for venom as with warlike people but pagan attempts to court the pleasure of the spirits of the elements, animals and fish. Yet as they progressed in tempo, the dancers and watchers became so filled with religious fervor they lost their native sense of emotional control and the ceremonies often became sensual orgies.

The Yuroks on the lower Klamath River had fewer dances but three were very vital to them—the Salmon Dance indoors in the spring, the Jumping Dance and White Deer Dance outdoors in the fall. The Tolowas, north and south of the mouth of the Smith River, celebrated the stranding of a dead whale on the beach by chanting and dancing with wild abandon around the odorous carcass and gorging on its rotten blubber.

They performed an Elk Dance when they snared or shot one of these animals with bow and arrow. Their men had a war dance which rivaled the savage ones of the plains, painting their bodies with gorgeously barbaric designs, brandishing weapons, setting up blood-curdling shrieks and cavorting in weird postures. The Priestess Dance, indulged in by a female healer or shaman, was an offering to the over-all spirit in which, by a nine-day fast and constant incantations, she brought herself into communication with the evil spirits and implored them to destroy certain witchcraft.

The Hupas, on the upper Trinity River and Redwood Creek, lent more color to their dances and performed more of them. Their White Deer Dance in which only men participated, was conducted to ensure good hunting and ample food during the winter. The hide of the white deer, of a value so high it could never be sold, had in fact a sacred significance and was handled with all reverence and care. When killed, every part of the animal was preserved. Head and neck were stuffed, tufts of red woodpecker scalps sewed on the ear tips, around the eyes and on a strip of skin hanging down from the mouth to resemble the tongue. During the dance several of these goodwill symbols were mounted on log poles and proper gestures made to the animal spirits.

With the Friendship Dance, the Hupas showed the act of welcome to visiting tribes or important individuals. The Puberty Dance commemorated the maturity of a girl in high tribal standing and made her eligible for marriage. The Dance of Peace was the Hupas' greatest celebration, symbolizing friendly relations with neighboring tribes. The dancers were two priestesses and twenty-five men, all gloriously arrayed, performing in a semicircular enclosure of wooden stakes in which a fire burned constantly. The women wore fur slips and many strings of shells; the men, tasseled deerskins with broad headbands or snowwhite buckskin headdresses brilliantly decorated with red and green woodpecker down.

The other villagers assembled outside the palisades. A solemn chant rose up from the dancers, the volume rising continually until the sounds became wild shrieks with legs and arms gyrating in all directions. Then suddenly the voices and actions would stop, the forest thrown into sudden silence again. This cycle was repeated hour by hour.

The White Deerskin Dance with the Karoks was pointedly a ritual to commemorate the renewal of the year, the beginning of the world. It was a celebration of appeasement, performed to prove to the spirits of earth and forest that the people were happy, held no ill feelings and expected no storms, fires, earthquakes, landslides or droughts. Early in the autumn all villages would be deserted and unprotected, all men, women and children taking to canoes on the Klamath River or walking on trails beside it, carrying the simple foods—dried salmon and acorn bread.

One man of the village was sent to the depths of the forest. He was called the "Kareya" man, chosen for his spiritual strength and physical stamina, a man fit to suffer anguish and plead compassion for the whole village. He started from his sweathouse and went to a solitary camp in the mountains. He built a fire and stayed by it all day and all night, praying for the prosperity of the people during the new year. At midnight he partook of a little food, a swallow or two of acorn soup. The next day he moved to another secluded spot and began another solitary vigil. For ten days, sleeping in a different place each night, always in deep solitude—except for an attendant to whom he never spoke—he ate only the thin acorn porridge and prostrated himself in suppliance before the guardian spirit of all.

The traveling pilgrims, meanwhile, had set up camp by the river in a pleasant meadow or grove where the good spirit was happy. Gradually, the people fell into festive mood and by nightfall, in the dark of the moon, some were chanting in a singsong tone or playing games for amusement and shell money, some sitting quietly in a circle around the fire. The younger and more active Karoks danced with long, leaping steps, changing their paces to slow walks. Then again, with the flames flickering on their faces, they fell into weird contortions of the savage dance, their tasseled deerskins flying, gaily colored headdresses bobbing and jerking. From deep in their throats came the deathly rattle of despair and supplication, moans of simulated pain, chantings and rantings more animal than human. When they spoke words, they formed no coherent sentences, but improvised under the excitement and emotional drive of the moment.

Then came the messenger from the the forest to warn the celebrants of the approach of the Kareya man who had been suffering for them and making their obeisances to the spirits. And the people fled as though from a terror because it was death to behold this "holy" man. As they scurried away, some hid in rock niches or fell into tangles of brush, the ones with small children wrapping them safely in reed blankets and skins. If any person should behold the forbidden sight, he prostrated himself in abject submission, offering shell money and paying whatever demanded even if it was death.

Gaunt and haggard, the spirit emissary appeared with his attendant at the hushed, deserted camp, perhaps so weak he must be borne in by the servant. An assembly chamber had been prepared for him and now the vassal helped him through the small hole in the side and sat him upon the sacred stool, before which a small fire was kindled. As the acrid, choking fumes curled up around him, he moaned and whimpered as though in the last stages of the death struggle.

When the spiritual communion was considered at an end hours later, the people returned. They came timidly but soon were forming and dressing for the great dance. In the early hours, the actions were controlled and conformed to studied gaiety, every person conscious of the gravity and solemnity of the occasion. The men arranged them-

A. W. ERICSON PHOTO, COURTESY MRS. PERCY L. BRYAN

Yurok House at Weitchpec

selves in a long line, dressed in all the finery they possessed from buckskin bandoliers, jingling strings of elk teeth and snail shells to tasseled pelts starred with woodpecker scalps. Some wore even fancier costumes with basketry on their heads, streams of grass or strips of skin and feathers hanging down their backs.

To the incantations of song and meaningless choralling, repeated over and over, there was a brandishing of obsidian blades and finest bows inlaid with sinew and bits of shells. In the center, three men led in the singing and dancing. Four others with headpieces of deer horns curling upward, danced in front of the Kareya man and all others. With flints in hand and whistles in mouth, they started toward each other, striking sparks and emitting shrill whistles. They passed each other and all the dancers.

Behind them glinted the jewelled headbands of the women in the reflected fire-light, their garments alive with strings of pink and purple abalone shells. And above all this animated splendor, the deer and raccoon heads with their stuffed necks were waved and undulated on long poles.

All night the dance continued—sometimes all the next day. There was a steady pounding of bare feet and the air was filled with a droning and humming, pierced at intervals with screams and shrieks. And then all sounds ceased. The Kareya man had appeared before them naked. All the dancers hid their faces as the holy one went to the fire and knelt in silent meditation. One dancer approached him reverently with a burning torch of pitch and he put on his clothes.

The dance continued but now all semblance of reverence was gone. It was as though the people realized the spirits had accepted their pleas and now they were free to let themselves go and return to normal pleasures. Dancers, tribesmen and their women, cast all reserve aside and launched themselves into an orgy of complete physical abandon. Their was no longer any rhythm or united effort. The dancers went into a frenzy, making wild postures and poses as it suited each one. And within minutes the scene had become the chaos of a mob—an obscene, sexual debauch. When, in utter exhaustion, the Karoks returned to their villages, they lit the fires in the assembly rooms and sweathouses that would not be allowed to expire until spring.

The Karok Half-Marriage

IN the damp darkness of the night several hundred years ago a young Karok Indian can be imagined sitting at the swelling base of a redwood tree and counting his string money. It does not take him long. He already knows he has but three strings of twelve and thirteen dentalium shells each. And he also realizes with sadness that his only other possessions of wealth are a yew hunting bow, well sinewed for strength yet which he has never learned to use properly, a few cedar arrows with dulled points, a salmon spear and a mangy coyote skin.

The Karok youth is well aware of the fact that these treasures are hardly more than the simple tools of keeping alive. But he wants much more than that. He wants a girl—one certain girl of the village. He has wanted her ever since she became a woman but has waited in the hope that his talks with the spirit of the wildcat will result in an increase of his strength and a desire to work harder at fishing and hunting so he can grow richer and buy her. But now he knows the girl's father will not sell her for three strings, perhaps not for three times three strings.

The youth creeps back into the smoky confines of the sweathouse where seven men of the village live and lies flat close to the fires so as not to be suffocated by the fumes. A hand touches his arm and he jerks up to see one of the older men on his knees, a look of scorn on the dark face where the fire glow catches it.

"This thing," the man is telling him, "that keeps you on the move at night like a porcupine. This woman. Everybody knows what they see. You are no good to anybody. Like a seal on the sand. Half dead. Her father knows you cannot buy her. Anybody but you would know what to do. Pay what you have and go to live with this woman. Where her father lives. You are no good here. You do not even get wood for the fire."

This voice seems to be coming out of the air instead of a man and the youth is more willing to believe it is his dead grandfather talking and not a man he stays with here in this sweathouse. But the voice speaks what is true and it makes him calm. At dawn he climbs up out of the earthen chamber and throws himself in the river, scrubbing himself with small branches as he has seen god-men do. Then he gathers up all his possessions including a woven waistband which he rarely bothers to wear and goes to the house where the girl lives with her sisters, father and mother. She is making acorn mush and waits for him to speak. Instead, he squats by the oval entrance to the cedar house and says nothing. He waits a long time before the father comes out.

This man is very dark, taller than most, and very strong. He has a big hunting bow in his hand, many arrows in the fine squirrel skin quiver with the tail left on. No, he says he does not want to talk to anybody about anything now but the youth can follow him up to where the small lake runs downhill and if by that time he has shot some food, he will sit down and talk. This is definitely not what the young suitor had in mind but he has no will to disagree.

Luckily for him, the father shoots several grouse and although he is hungry he takes time to listen to what this young villager has to say. When he hears the words, he spits on the earth and rubs the place with his bare foot.

Blind Yurok Woman Making Fish Trap—Trinidad River

"My daughter—eight strings. She is not worth more than seven but she belongs to me and I will sell her for what I want. If I do not sell her to you, she will be worth one string less every spring. Now you have only three strings and are not worth more than that. You cannot have her for full wife. Only half. You live in my house, hunt and fish for me. If my daughter says you clean fish, that is what you do."

And that is what the youth does—as other lovesick or lazy Karoks and neighboring tribesmen did before and after him. The half-marriage was an established custom, somewhat common, especially where wealthy men wanted more wealth and were able to keep their daughters too. They had another menial around the house, the daughters had the advantages of being married with the ease and comfort they were used to. Rich men often arranged this type of marriage, so convenient to their well-being.

It was no bed of roses for the husband and only the inadequate and indolent consented to it. This man was almost a slave, free only of the stigma of slavery, to both his wife and her father. He was their property as were his children. He had few rights as an individual, little voice in the running of his family. He could not beat his wife without paying money which he had little chance of accumulating. If by some lucky chance he killed a bear or an elk, his father-in-law took possession of it immediately and no doubt the father-in-law took all proper steps to keep an arrow out of his back or a rock from falling on his head.

A. W. ERICSON PHOTOS, COURTESY MRS. PERCY L. BRYAN

White Deerskin Dancers—Hupa

A. W. ERICSON PHOTOS, COURTESY MRS. PERCY L. BRYAN

White Deerskin Dance—Hupa

162

Tolowa Indian—Lake Earl

EDWARD L. CURTIS PHOTOS COURTESY
CHARLES E. LAURIAT CO.

Yurok Canoe on Trinity River

Klamath Woman

Klamath Headdress of Tule Stems

A. W. ERICSON PHOTOS
COURTESY MRS. PERCY L. BRYAN

*Yurok Weaver
on Mad River*

Hupa Fisherman

*Yurok with Double-
Pointed Spear*

EDWARD L. CURTIS PHOTO COURTESY
CHARLES E. LAURIAT CO.

A. W. ERICSON PHOTOS
COURTESY MRS. PERCY L. BRYAN

Hupas and Sweathouse

Tolowa Girl—Lake Earl

SISKIYOU CO. HISTORICAL SOC.

Shasta House

*Shasta Sweathouse—
Klamath River*

LESLIE D. HYDE, SISKIYOU CO.
HISTORICAL SOC.

Karok Woman and Child

Karoks Ready for Jumping Dan

*Klamath Warrior
in Plains
Indian Costume*

EDWARD L. CURTIS PHOTO COURTESY
CHARLES E. LAURIAT CO.

BIBLIOGRAPHY

Tribes of California.
> Stephen Powers; North American Ethnology.   Vol. III.

Indian Legends of the Pacific Northwest.
> Ella E. Clark.

Indians of Canada.
> National Museum of Canada.   Bulletin 65.

California Indians.
> R. F. Heizer and M. A. Whipple.

The Four Ages of Tsurai.
> Robert F. Heizer and John E. Mills.

Indians of the Northwest Coast.
> Phillip Drucker.

Indians of the Urban Northwest.
> Marian W. Smith.

The Makah Indians.
> Elizabeth Colson.

Indians of Puget Sound.
> Haeberlin and Gunther.

Narrative of John R. Jewett.

British Columbia Heritage Series.
> Vols. 1, 2, 4, 5, 6, 7, 10.

Journal of John Work.
> Archives of British Columbia.

Smoke From Their Fires.
> Clellan S. Ford.

Siwash—Their Life, Legends and Tales.
> J. A. Costello.

Tribes of the Columbia Valley.
> Albert B. Lewis.

Tribes of Western Washington and Northwest Oregon.
> George Gibbs, M.D.

Totem Poles.
> Vols. 1 and 2.   Marius Barbeau.

The Modern Growth of the Totem Pole on the Pacific Coast.
> Marius Barbeau.

In the Wake of the War Canoe.
> W. H. Collison.

INDEX